THE ART OF SAVING MONEY

THE ART OF SAVING MONEY

Grow Rich with the Money Monk

MANOJ ARORA

An imprint of
Srishti Publishers & Distributors

Srishti Publishers & Distributors
A unit of AJR Publishing LLP
212A, Peacock Lane
Shahpur Jat, New Delhi – 110 049

editorial@srishtipublishers.com

First published by Bold,
an imprint of Srishti Publishers & Distributors in 2025

10 9 8 7 6 5

Printed and bound in India.

A book is not written from your mind, but your heart.

And HE is the only one who can ignite your heart.

Contents

Preface

THE SECRET ALPHA

My NGO, Kalpavriksha, which was started with the intent of reducing air pollution by planting trees, was one of my dream projects after I became financially free, and has given us many reasons to smile. Other than purifying the air we breathe and giving us a reason to live, nature teaches us lessons at every step of our lives. I have personally learnt a lot from trees and nature just by observing how they respond to conditions, how they propagate, protect themselves, and how they flourish.

One such observation was during a tree plantation project in an abandoned park, or rather a vacant plot abandoned by the municipality, which was close to our house. To the credit of the municipality, however, this piece of land had a neatly constructed footpath piercing right through it from the entrance to the exit.

Both the sides of the footpath were supposed to have trees and grass but then, since no one seemed to care for the piece of land, both sides of the footpath were barren when Kalpavriksha took over and started the project. The footpath that ran through the plot was used by pedestrians to cross through to the other side of this mini-park, which led to the local market.

The left half of the area, was primarily used by school-going kids for playing local gulley cricket, especially in the winters, while the area on the right was untouched and had grown wild.

Kalpavriksha took the initiative to plant trees and transform the barren land. We convinced the budding cricketers to move to a new location, and after clearing the area, seventy-five native trees were planted in the mini-park, almost equally on both sides of the footpath.

But as you would appreciate, planting the trees is the easiest part of the journey. It is usually not more than a day's work. It's the protection of the planted trees from stray animals and humans, regular watering, and nurturing that not only takes time, but also takes immense effort and monumental patience before the trees become big enough to be handed over to nature.

Usually, we spend about a couple of years caring for every tree, and depending on their growth, we can leave them to nature from thereon. However, we had a strange experience during this project, and from these strange experiences came new lessons. Almost half of the trees were stunted, even though it had been three years since they had been planted. Meanwhile, the other half had a natural and decent growth and were ready to be handed over to nature. We were unable to bring the project to an end because of the trees, which were not growing well despite our best efforts.

We were all very surprised by this difference in the growth of trees, even though they were located at the same location, had the same exposure to soil and fertilisers, sunlight, watering, and were cared for by the same set of volunteers.

This strange phenomenon kept us puzzled for a long time. Then, one day, during my nth visit to the site, it struck me.

Almost all the trees with stunted growth were located on the left side of the footpath. Though the soil, watering, and sunlight were identical, there was a big difference between the two sides of the footpath.

The soil on the left side of the footpath had become hard because the children who used to play cricket had been romping on it day in and day out for many years. On the other hand, the soil on the right side of the footpath was loose, giving it the ability to absorb much more, much faster. We were feeding the soil on both sides of the park with the same amount of water and fertilizers, but what we fed was not what all the plants were receiving.

While some soil density is necessary for soil structure and stability, excessive density significantly hinders nutrient absorption by affecting water movement, root growth, microbial activity, and nutrient availability. And that was precisely what was happening to the trees on the left side of the footpath.

The plants were getting what could seep through from the soil to the roots. We could keep watering a tree for an entire lifetime, but if the soil is covered with concrete, the roots get zilch, and the tree will obviously not grow.

- *What makes a tree grow is not what it is fed with, but what it is ultimately able to take in, what it absorbs.* And the right level of soil density was the secret for the trees to absorb the right nutrients and water.
- The soil density is the **Secret Alpha** for nutrient absorption by the trees, ultimately leading to better growth.

***

I have quite a large number of plants in my terrace garden. I water each of those plants myself and also monitor the progress of their growth. The water pipe I use to water the plants is not long enough. While the plants that are in direct reach of the water pipe are watered directly on the soil, the ones that are out of reach are usually sprinkled with water on their leaves from a fair distance through water pressure created by squeezing the pipe outlet.

If I continue to do this for a few weeks, that is, watering some plants directly on the soil and sprinkling some of them with water on their leaves, can you now guess which set of plants would grow better? Of course, we are assuming all other conditions like sunlight, manure, soil quality, soil density and so on generally remain the same.

Yes, there is a definite difference in their growth, flowering, and in everything else that one can observe. So, make a guess – which category of plants grows better, the ones which are watered directly on the soil and happen to get more water, or the ones whose leaves are sprinkled with water, and which happen to get relatively less water since some of it gets spilled?

Common sense says that the plants which get more water should grow more. But the surprising bit is that the reality turns out to be precisely opposite. The ones on which water was sprinkled are growing much better than the other category of plants, watered directly into the soil.

So why did this happen?

After seeing this phenomenon work consistently, and after a bit of research, I found out the reason. The leaves of the plants that are sprinkled with water become clean of dust and pollution. As such, they can absorb the natural sunlight much better, resulting in more efficient photosynthesis and hence have more food prepared for themselves, ultimately resulting in better growth.

And this is after the fact that these plants that grew more were receiving relatively less water. The sunlight they were receiving, and all other factors, were the same as those of other plants that didn't grow as well.

After observing this pattern over many seasons, I came to the following conclusion:

- *What makes a plant grow is not how much sunlight it receives, but what it ultimately takes in, or what it absorbs.* The cleaner the leaf, the more sunlight it can absorb.
- The leaf cleanliness is the **Secret Alpha** for sunlight absorption, ultimately leading to better growth.

***

A few years back, my wife was going through generic symptoms characterised by a tingling sensation around her mouth, lack of energy, as well as repeated dental issues. We tried many home remedies to address these issues individually, but in vain.

So, after a few months of failed attempts at home, we decided to meet our family doctor. After going through all the symptoms that we described, the doctor suggested we test for calcium deficiency. We were also able to correlate the calcium deficiency to the fact that she had suffered fractures many times in the past, which is usually considered a result of weak bones.

We came back home, satisfied with the fact that now we knew the root cause of the issue, and were now hoping for a quick resolution. We made some changes to our diet. We added more milk, cheese, nuts and seeds, as well as lentils and pulses. And we hoped that additional calcium intake would help us overcome the issues over time. We continued for quite a while, but even after many months, the impact was negligible.

Her symptoms were not getting better. That is when we decided to take calcium supplements. We went to a pharmacy near our house, and since we did not have a prescription, and calcium was available as an over-the-counter tablet, we didn't bother to call our doctor, and just picked one of the brands.

We continued the calcium tablets for a few weeks but again there was hardly any significant improvement in her symptoms.

It became evident the tablets were not really helping, so we reached out to our family doctor again.

After hearing our saga, he asked us to get my wife's Vitamin D levels tested. We did as advised and were shocked to see the test report. Her Vitamin D levels were around 9 ng/ml. The normal range is somewhere between 30 and 100 ng/ml. So, that meant she was highly deficient in Vitamin D.

We looped back to our doctor, and he suggested we take some Vitamin D tablets along with her calcium tablets, but at the same time, he was very clear that her symptoms had nothing to do with Vitamin D deficiency but only with calcium deficiency.

We didn't argue much and just followed his advice, and within a couple of weeks, the symptoms eased. After a few months, she was back to living her best, vibrant and active life.

A few days later, just out of curiosity, and to thank our doctor, I called him and checked with him on why he asked us to check for Vitamin D levels if he strongly believed that all the symptoms were only because of calcium deficiency. And his response startled me, yet again.

Our doctor explained that Vitamin D was the agent that was needed by our body to absorb calcium and since my spouse was highly deficient in Vitamin D levels, her calcium intake was getting wasted and thrown out of the body with very little actually getting absorbed. Naturally, her symptoms were not showing any signs of improvement.

I came back home and explained this to my spouse. And after much reflection, I concluded the following:

- *What matters is not how much calcium our body is fed with, but what it ultimately takes in, or what it absorbs.* And Vitamin D helps the body absorb appropriate amounts of calcium.

- Vitamin D is the **Secret Alpha** for calcium absorption in our body, ultimately leading to proper body functions.

***

The total power from the sun that reaches earth is about 174 petawatts. Now, for those who are not aware, 1 petawatt = 10^{15} watts or 1,000,000,000,000,000 watts. To put this figure in perspective, it's forty times more than the total global electricity consumption, and equivalent to the output of millions of nuclear power plants. It's a scale that exceeds most energy systems we work with on earth.

Earth and its atmosphere absorb most of this energy. Have you ever thought what would happen if this immense energy were not absorbed by the earth? Let me give you a perspective.

Within a few days, the earth's surface could drop to -100°C or colder. After a few months, the earth's average temperature could approach -200°C or lower. Life would struggle to survive in such extreme conditions, as water would freeze, and most biological processes would halt. The atmosphere itself would begin to freeze and condense, especially gases like oxygen and nitrogen, which would form solid or liquid states under extremely cold temperatures. This would remove the protective blanket of air we rely on for life.

In essence, life would cease to exist.

Absorption of heat by the earth and its atmosphere is thus essential for our survival on this planet. So, what helps earth absorb this heat and keep life going? When this heat energy reaches earth, part of it is absorbed by the atmosphere, while the rest of it passes through to the earth's surface. Greenhouse gases like water vapour, carbon dioxide, methane, and nitrous oxide absorb infrared radiation from the earth's surface and then re-radiate it in all directions, including back toward the earth's surface. This helps to keep the planet warm by reducing heat loss to space.

On earth's surface, the solar radiation is absorbed by land, oceans, and vegetation and converted into heat. This heat raises the temperature of the land and water, which in turn heats the air above the surface.

Once heat is absorbed by the surface (particularly the oceans), it is transported around the globe by ocean currents. These currents circulate warm water from the equator toward the poles, helping to distribute heat more evenly across the planet.

There are many more ecosystem processes that help the earth stay warm and ensure we survive.

- *What matters is not how much heat our planet is fed with, but what it ultimately takes in, or what it absorbs, that ensures life on the planet.* The entire ecosystem around the earth helps it absorb this heat and helps us survive.
- Earth's ecosystem is the **Secret Alpha** for heat absorption by earth, ultimately leading to our survival on this planet.

***

There are endless instances of such secret alphas around us. It's just that I have been noticing more of them of late.

When fifty students study in a class, and the same teacher is teaching all fifty students in precisely the same way, yet why is it that some students absorb more, some less, and some nothing. It does not matter what is being taught by the teacher. What matters is what is being absorbed by the students. The alpha factor in this case could be the attention the student is paying in class.

If we try to pour water into a bottle that has its lid on, then nothing goes in, irrespective of the amount of water that is poured over the bottle. The lid is the alpha factor that decides how much water goes in from the water that is poured.

Another instance is when you make tea for your spouse and put just the right amount of sugar in it before serving it to him or her. But if you have not stirred the cup after putting the sugar in it, they are likely to reject the cup. That is because the amount of sugar you put in the cup does not matter. What matters is how much of that sugar gets absorbed in the tea. Stirring the teacup is the alpha factor in this case. The more you stir, the better the absorption is.

Diabetes is a raging new world problem. Those who are dealing with it and managing it well understand that apart from your eating habits, stress, and sleep, what matters the most in managing your blood sugar levels is exercise. But why? Because when we exercise, the muscles and cells need more sugar to sustain the energy needed to exercise. So, our body cells absorb this additional sugar from our blood, leading to better-managed blood sugar levels. So, the alpha factor here is exercise, which helps better absorption of sugar into your body cells.

The key is not what 'comes in', but what 'stays in', or what gets 'absorbed'.

Do not get me wrong here. Without anything coming in, nothing gets absorbed. So, what comes in is surely important, but that alone is futile.

What gets absorbed, or what stays in, is what makes the real impact. The Secret Alpha is what helps the incoming entity to be absorbed. And if every sphere of life depends on this 'Secret Alpha', how can personal finance be any different?

I have met and personally interacted with so many professionals, engineers, doctors, chartered accountants, teachers, business folks, CFOs and other CXOs working in some of the best companies across the globe and earning more than handsome salaries. They are the top 1 per cent income earners in India. Such impressive salaries are a testimony to the times we live in, the opportunities available in this digital age, and of course, the hard work, focus and perseverance of these professionals in their respective domains.

But despite such respectable salaries, almost all of them struggle to build massive wealth. You may not believe this, but I see this every day, since I advise them on their portfolios and on investing strategies. I know their incomes, and I also know their net worth. In most cases, the net worth is not enough to fund their retired lives.

And the reason for this lack of wealth creation is no different from what we have seen so far.

What matters is not how much money comes in, but what is ultimately taken in, or what it absorbed.

Most of those who earn fancy incomes also have equally fancy show-offs – be it cars and houses, or parties and gadgets. They all raise their standard of living as per their incomes. They forget that the income will stop one day, in fact it can even stop abruptly any day. It will be tough for them to survive a few months without active income – forget about the freedom from the necessity to keep earning to support their lifestyle.

You might feel that if they hire good financial advisers, they can grow their wealth faster, but wealth will grow only after they save (or absorb) money and have enough investible surplus that can be invested for optimal returns. The first step in creating wealth is income, and the second most vital step is saving, or absorption of that income.

Without saving, there are no investments, and without investments, there are no returns.

Let me illustrate my point with the following example. Rohit has an income of ₹ 2 lakhs per month, and Arun has an income of ₹ 1 lakh per month. With this much information, we would obviously tend to believe that the chances of Rohit getting wealthier is far more than that of Arun.

But then, what matters more is the absorption of this income.

Rohit has a savings ratio of 10 per cent. So, from an income of ₹ 2 lakhs, Rohit is able to save and invest ₹ 20,000 every month. Arun, on the other hand, has a savings ratio of 30 per cent. So, from an income of ₹ 1 lakh, he is able to save and invest ₹ 30,000 every month.

Now, who do you think has a better chance of getting wealthier?

Of course, it does not take rocket science to conclude that the chances of Arun getting wealthier are far higher now, despite having half the income. We are making an obvious assumption that both invest whatever they save, and both derive similar returns from their invested money.

So, while income is important, it is not the most important element in wealth creation. What matters at the end of the day is what gets absorbed or saved from that income. While I understood very clearly that saving is what matters and not the income, I was still struggling to understand what the Secret Alpha for high savings could be. There must be one, for sure. If there is a Secret Alpha everywhere else in nature, there must be one in personal finance. Just that, I didn't know what it was.

I was struggling with this question.

What is the Secret Alpha that helps us absorb more income, so that we can invest more and get wealthier faster? Just hold it. Have patience. I struggled with this for many years, and you are getting it on a platter? How unfair.

I am sharing all these life observations about the Secret Alpha, not because they are new inventions on this planet, but because I myself have started to observe life more carefully around me and have started creating patterns more closely.

The power of observation and the ability to create patterns is an incredible power. Most scientists and engineers often rely on observation and patterns in data to discover new phenomena or troubleshoot issues. When we observe something carefully, we can also spot when something doesn't fit the usual pattern, which can be crucial for identifying problems or opportunities.

Observing patterns in the world around us is the mother of creativity. I say this because creativity is not about creating new stuff. Creativity often involves combining ideas or elements in new ways. By observing different aspects of life – whether it's nature, art, or technology – we can create new patterns or connections between seemingly unrelated things. Many breakthroughs in science and art have come from recognising hidden patterns in existing knowledge.

These abilities to observe carefully and create patterns have made me more insightful, adaptable, and capable of navigating the complexities of daily life and work.

But the interesting point is that I was not always like this, and neither was Varun, my bosom pal. It all changed after we attended the five-day programme by none other than the Money Monk. (We now refer to him as MM in our conversations.)

We were introduced to the idea of 'Secret Alpha' in a get-together at our common friend's place where we happened to meet MM by chance. This was more than ten years ago. As MM explained the idea to us, he caught our interest, and we had our own set of questions which none of us hesitated to ask.

What could have helped Arun absorb/save more than Rohit?

What was the Secret Alpha for Arun?

Was there one alpha factor or a set of alpha factors? Can all those alpha factors be listed down?

If all of us can get access to those 'secret' alpha factors, can we use those to create massive wealth for ourselves and our families? If there are such Secret Alpha factors, then why are people not focused on them to absorb and save more?

Why are most people focused on just earning more?

I asked MM all these questions on the sidelines of this get-together and then waited patiently for his answers.

MM responded, "The reason is that people don't know the power of absorption, and they don't know how to absorb more while leading a happy and fulfilling life. They do not know that such a power exists. They have never observed nature carefully, probably due to a lack of time to observe natural patterns. They just know how to earn, and they keep earning for their entire life. And then end up frustrated with not having enough. How will they have enough when their absorption rate is so low?"

"Okay, I get that completely, however, I also have another observation," commented Varun, and the topic deviated from my question.

"Sure... go ahead, Varun."

"I agree that most people are focused on just earning more to get rich. But there are many more who are focused on getting better returns from whatever they can save, rather than trying to save or absorb more. Is it not good to have more returns from whatever we have absorbed?" asked Varun.

"Yes, of course, wealth can be amassed with either of the strategies, i.e., getting higher returns on a given principal amount or getting moderate returns on a higher principal amount, or even a combination of these two. But what people do not appreciate enough is that getting higher returns entails taking higher risks, while higher principal accumulation entails zero additional risk. And this matters in the long run, because at some point, the risk will play out."

"Interesting. I never thought about it from the risk angle. Absorbing or saving more can definitely create risk-free wealth," Varun commented.

"Achieving higher returns is also a tool for many advisers to attract new clients. Because the whole point is that everyone is in a hurry to get rich without paying any price for wealth accumulation."

"Is there anything wrong with trying to get rich quickly?" I asked MM.

"No, there is absolutely nothing wrong, but people are just in the wrong vehicle if they want to get rich quickly. Aiming for high returns to get rich quickly is very risky. They can go bankrupt as well. Many actually do," responded MM.

"Yes, I know of a few who invested in high-risk, high-reward investments and went bankrupt. You remember Kartik, our neighbour? He lost almost everything investing in some high-risk scheme." Varun looked at me while agreeing with MM.

"Oh, I wasn't aware," I responded.

Varun looked back at MM and asked, "So, what is the best way to get rich quickly, according to you?"

"Spend less, save more, invest more. What gets absorbed is going to create long-term risk-free wealth for you," MM reiterated.

"Really? Spending less, saving more? All this sounds rather old-fashioned, though," I responded.

"Do you want to get rich or sound fashionable?" came the response from MM.

"Ha ha... yes, getting rich is way better!" both Varun and I agreed wholeheartedly.

"But I am back to my first question. How do we save more? I mean, we do not want to ruin our lifestyle or family lives just to save more. We are already trying our best," I resisted the idea.

"So, if both of you are serious about getting rich and that too risk-free, then you guys should plan to attend our January session. That might be the last one I will be conducting. I will share with you the 'secret alphas' to saving more and getting rich quickly without taking an iota of any additional risk."

Both Varun and I looked at each other before I said, "Done deal then, January it is!"

We were convinced by the idea of the Secret Alpha which would make us wealthy, not only quickly, but without taking any risk. And we waited eagerly for MM's January session.

Day 0

WALKING DOWN

"I have to leave early in the morning," I told Kritika over the dinner table, as we were winding up our meal after an evening walk.

"Oh, but your sessions will start only in the evening, no?" she inquired.

"Yeah, Kritu, but it is a three-hour drive through the outskirts of the city, and then it's a long walk for about an hour. So, it will take almost half a day to just reach there. And Varun and I are also planning to make a pit stop at our friend Kishore's house for lunch. It has been a long time since we met. So, it's better I leave early to avoid the traffic as well," I tried to justify the early start.

"That makes sense. Can't afford to get stuck in traffic. Fine. So, where are you meeting Varun?" she asked.

"We will drive separately and meet at Nathu point. We will leave our cars at Kishore's house for the next five days, have lunch and meet his family, and then we will walk together to the venue."

"How long will you be gone, Manish?"

"It is a five-day programme. Will be back on Monday."

"Your Tarun Zombie gave you leave for the entire week? I am a bit surprised. How will his department survive without you?" Kritika joked.

She knew my boss, Tarun, very well. Her question was not without merit. My boss was a workaholic and expected the same from everyone in the team.

"No, no, dear... he approved only three days' leave. Will bunk the remaining days."

"Oh! Mind you, don't lose your job for this Money Monk..."

"Tarun Zombie can't afford to fire me," I tried to laugh it out. "And this Monk seems to be very unique."

"Really?"

"Yeah, I have heard so much about him. I must meet him. There is something special about this guy."

"Okay, but monks are in the news nowadays for wrong reasons more than right."

"I know. But he is special, Kritika. You know Kavita, right? She had been to the sessions. Lokesh was there a few weeks back as well. They said that spending a week there was a life-elevating experience. Their perspective towards life, money, savings, investing – everything has undergone a paradigm shift."

"I really hope so... okay Manish, wish you luck. I am sure you are going to miss my food, though."

"Yeah, true. It will mostly be raw fruits and vegetables there, I've heard."

"I am going to miss you a lot, Manish. I haven't stayed without you for so many days at a stretch."

"Yeah, that is true. I am going to miss you too, darling. I told you that there is a family programme option as well. You can join me if you are willing, Kritika."

"I am not so keen on learning this art of saving money. Saving is your headache. I am an expert at spending money, no?"

Both of us had a good laugh.

Kritika had been such a blessing in my life. She had never ever thought twice about her decision to quit her career and dedicate the best part of her life to our daughters, while I was busy working. And now she was going to manage everything while I would be away – their school, homework, activities, everything. It was a tough, thankless job with no compensation in any form.

She deserved more, much more than what I was giving her. She deserved a lot of my time. She deserved more of my love. And of course, she loved shopping and deserved much more money than I could afford to give her. She never complained, but I know what excited her the most.

And the less I talk about my sweet little angels, the better. Chirpy, smart, intelligent – they were just the perfect beings Kritika and I wanted in our lives. We had been so blessed. Parenting had obviously not been easy, but it had been extremely worthwhile so far. I just wish I had more time to spend with each one of them. I wish I could take them more often on international trips. I wish.... and I had been wishing for a long time. My aspirations were high, but was it a crime to have high aspirations?

What could I do to fulfil these high aspirations? The programme on 'The Art of Saving Money' was my small hope that I could achieve financial freedom faster, and much sooner than my retirement. I yearned to go on international trips with my girls before unstoppable time separated us, before they went off to different cities, countries and continents to pursue the careers and jobs of their dreams; before Kritika and I lost the ability or energy to dance, climb or swim; before fate played any unexpected role; before the ever growing corporate stress and politics took its toll on my health; and before I realised that while I could trade my time for money, that all the money in the world was not enough to buy even a single moment of time once it was up!

Life is fragile but also beautiful. I wanted to live it fully, with the ones I loved and cared for. Give me a chance, life. Give me a chance. I could stress more to earn more. I had been doing it for decades now, but I was exhausted. Even if I earned more, I just couldn't seem to save more. Whether it was cost inflation, Lifestyle Inflation or whatever else, I didn't know and I didn't care. I wanted to be shown a way, and I would do anything for my freedom.

This programme had given me some hope. And I would do my best to latch on to this hope and try to make the best out of it. I slept with these thoughts and woke up with my alarm going off.

Kritika was still asleep. I got ready, whispered in her ears that I was leaving, kissed her goodbye, and looked at her beautiful and calm face for one last time before leaving. She deserved more of me. I deserved more of her.

And I walked down the stairs towards my car. I set up Google Maps, texted Varun, and finally began the exciting trip. Once I was out of the parking lot on the lane towards the main road, and then on the highway, I started to drive towards the city outskirts. It was very early in the morning. In a city like Bengaluru, one can only enjoy a serene drive this time of the day, before the maddening corporate race induced unbearable traffic jams.

A fresh and cool breeze welcomed me on the highway. I switched off the AC and opened the windows, tuned the Amazon Music app to play one of my favourite freedom songs that I wrote just for such times....

Money's not the master, I ride my fate,
Stackin' little wins, now my life feels great.
No 9-to-5 chains, just open skies,
Dreams in my heart and fire in my eyes.
Every mile I drive, I'm breakin' free,
Financial freedom – that's the road for me!

Lost in my own dreams, with the freedom song on repeat mode,

I didn't realise I had arrived at the meeting point. I wanted the drive to go on and on, forever. Dreams are like that, I suppose.

"Hey Varun! Good morning, buddy. Where have you reached?" I called Varun to check.

"Good morning. Just ten minutes, buddy and I should be there," responded Varun.

"Okay, I have reached Nathu point, and I am standing in front of DBS school. It's adjacent to Kishore's bungalow. Once you reach, we'll go together to Kishore's."

"Yeah sure, will be there soon."

It probably took him less than ten minutes, but I lived all my dreams in those ten minutes, yet again. I have lived it again and again, hundreds of times, in my mind. The manifestation of my dreams was all that was pending.

"Why did you come in these shoes? I am sure you know that we will have to walk for an hour, Manish," remarked Varun when he looked at my semi-casual shoes.

"I plan to walk barefoot when we walk towards the resort," I responded with a strange sense of confidence.

"What's this new fascination with walking barefoot, man?"

"No, it is not fascination, buddy. Actually, one of my friends told me that walking barefoot is a natural acupressure technique and it helps with the general upkeep of our health."

"Hmmm... you are very focused on your health these days, huh?"

"What to do, buddy? I am forced to."

"Why? Is everything okay?" asked Varun.

"Okay, in general, but there is so much work pressure and no major savings. The kids are growing up, and everything is becoming so costly. This seems to be causing undue stress and impacting my health, man."

"That is true... it's the same story almost everywhere. Let's drive down to our ultra successful friend's house and have a more meaningful chat there. Let's see what he has to say," Varun said as he got into his car, and we proceeded to the bungalow's parking lot.

Kishore, our classmate from the schooldays, was probably one of the most successful guys from our batch. Not only was he the school topper, he was an IIT, IIM-qualified guy, he had worked for Google for almost ten years in the US. He had a great family, and was now settled in India in a lavish bungalow. This was surely only one of the properties he owned across the globe.

We always knew that he led a lavish lifestyle, but it was a completely different feeling as we parked our respective hatchback cars next to his BMW, Lamborghini and Mercedes A-Class.

"This is what I want to be..." said Varun, as we walked out of the parking lot towards the bungalow.

"Yeah, man... we seem so insignificant in front of him, no?" I agreed with Varun.

"True, what else does a person want in life? He must be the happiest among all our friends."

"Yeah, I do not know whether it was the right decision to meet Kishore before going to the resort"

"Why do you say so, Varun? He is our buddy."

"Yeah, but I get an inferiority complex here. It seems that we have been utter failures in life."

I did not say anything. But the fact that I was also feeling inferior could not be denied. We just moved along.

Kishore was aware that we would be visiting him that day. We didn't confirm the exact timings, though. We never felt the need, as he was one of our best friends in school. We have always been close buddies, so we took the leverage of walking in at our chosen time.

As we approached the door and were about to ring the bell, we heard screaming and shouting from inside the house. I looked at Varun, and we halted. We waited for a couple of minutes in the hope that it would stop, but it continued unabated.

"Should we go back?" I asked Varun.

"No, I don't think so. I hope everything is okay. Maybe someone inside needs some help."

"So, should I ring the bell?"

"Yeah, go ahead, man," Varun said hurriedly as the screaming only got louder.

I suddenly saw the gardener around the house. As I inquired about the noise, he smiled and told me that it was a daily affair.

"Do not worry. You can go inside," said the gardener nonchalantly.

I gathered my courage and went ahead to ring the bell. The shouting and screaming continued. We waited at the door till a helper came and unlocked the door. After an introduction, he asked us to wait at the door as he went inside.

After a while, the shouting finally stopped. The helper returned, and we followed him as he guided us to the drawing room.

And what a drawing room it was. This one room was probably two times the size of our entire house – it housed a massive chandelier, a projector TV, elegant sofas, a small meeting table at the side, a gigantic library along the other wall, and a string of helpers preparing to serve the most elegant snacks.

"What will you have, sir? Tea or coffee? Hot or cold? With or without sugar?"

"We are fine, thank you. We just want to meet our friend Mr Kishore."

"Yes, I have informed sir. He should be here any time. Until then, should I get you something?"

"No, it is fine. Varun, do you want something?"

"No, not right now. Thanks."

The helper kept glasses of water in front of us and went off. We picked up a few magazines as we waited. Five minutes later, we saw Kishore coming down the stairs. We were seeing him after a decade. And how he had changed. He had become bald and looked dispirited, but managed to smile as he saw us.

"Hey buddies..." he raced towards us with open arms.

We all hugged each other tightly. It has been quite a while since we had met last, but that hug rekindled some of the nostalgic and cherished memories of school life.

"Hey Kishore... what success man! Congrats, buddy!" Varun opened up the conversation, gesturing towards his mammoth bungalow.

"Thanks, man... how have you guys been?"

"Well, we are carrying on, unlike you. You seem to be thriving. You are the dream so many of us are striving for," I responded.

And we chatted on and on about our lives, families, hobbies, and health. Before we knew it, it was almost lunch time. And as expected, lunch was elaborate and sumptuous. Both Varun and I stuffed ourselves. I do not remember ever having had such a lavish lunch, not even in a restaurant.

We returned to the sofa in the drawing room and continued our discussion.

"Where is Ananya? Isn't she home? We haven't even met her," I had to ask Kishore.

"She is fine. She is upstairs... a bit busy," Kishore responded with a frown.

I found it strange that she hadn't come down to meet us.

"All okay, buddy?" I asked.

Kishore came forward and hugged me tightly. I couldn't see what was forthcoming. Something was surely out of place.

Before I could ask what was wrong, I felt his racking sobs on my chest. Varun and I were shocked and had no clue how to react. He kept crying for more than five minutes. We did nothing except keep asking him if everything was fine and whether he or Ananya needed any help.

"Sorry, guys. I am spoiling your day with all this," he tried to gather himself.

"No, you are not. What are friends for? What is the issue? Is Ananya fine?"

"Yeah, she is fine."

"Then what's the problem, man? C'mon, please tell us."

And then he revealed what was even more shocking than seeing our friend crying.

"We are bankrupt."

"Who is bankrupt?" I asked.

"We – Ananya and I."

"C'mon, don't joke."

"Yes, that is the bitter truth. We have to sell all of this to pay our dues – our bungalow, cars, everything. Ananya and I keep having fights with each other on financial issues and keep blaming each other for this mess. It is very stressful, man. We will be moving to a two-bedroom apartment next year, and we hope that either of us is able to get a job to take care of our kids. Our kids don't even know about all this yet. It's tough... very tough..."

And Kishore started crying again with his hands over his face. He was unable to face us, and unable to face his own crashing image – an image that was created by the society around him. Varun and I were numb and didn't know how to react.

We gave Kishore the time that he needed.

"How did this happen, man? How can someone as smart as you land in such a financial mess?" Varun finally asked.

"We were always earning well, both in the US and India."

"Yeah, that is what surprises us. We know that you were one of the most successful among all of us. Then where did you go wrong?"

"We were earning well, but we were also spending well. Parties, clubs, cars, massive bungalow – the upkeep of this lifestyle was getting out of hand, and then, I lost my job out of the blue."

"Oh, this happened in India?"

"Yes, just a couple of years back."

"Oh... we didn't know that."

"Yeah, we thought we'd still be able to manage with Ananya's income. We were dependent on only one income. Our income was down to less than half, but our expenses didn't come down, even when we tried. We could not do away with our lavish lifestyle. Ananya kept telling me that we were stretching ourselves thin and we should sell a few of our cars and move to a smaller bungalow, but you know, a man's ego could never agree to this. Debts kept piling, the love between us was lost, and today, we are at a point where we do not have a choice but to move to a two-bedroom apartment. Hopefully, we can manage with Ananya's salary. I am still searching for a job," he shook his head in despair.

"Our biggest mistake was that we did not have any savings... any assets upon which we could bank in times of distress. We kept spending whatever we earned recklessly. And that lavish lifestyle has come crashing down now. I am unable to face Ananya. I am dependent on her income, yet I keep yelling at her...."

And he began sobbing profusely again.

After a while, he composed himself, and we tried our best to console him.

"Kishore, I understand, but you must look forward in life. You are looking for a job. You will get one sooner or later. Then things will start looking better. Do not worry. It is just a bad phase. This, too, shall pass."

"I am hoping for the best, too, but I'll never get the salary I was getting earlier. The industry is changing, and I will never have the same lifestyle. And I think I deserve this punishment for not being wise enough to save money; not being sane enough to understand Ananya; and for being stupid enough to follow the herd mentality of chasing a grander lifestyle than was needed or was affordable. Today, I neither have any style nor any life," he concluded with a sigh.

"The best of the people go through tough times. Knowing you, you will surely come out of it. Is there anything any of us can do to help? Please do not hesitate to tell us. We are old-time buddies and are always there for you," I said.

"No man, that's okay. Let me go through what I deserve. I have never shared this with anyone outside our family. You are the first ones. But I must ask for a favour."

"Sure... please go ahead and tell us," Varun patted his shoulder reassuringly.

"Do not let anyone else know about this. My ego is not resilient enough to handle the many opinions around me."

Varun and I looked at each other and committed, "You have our word."

"Thanks, buddies. I will have to leave for a job interview in the next few minutes. You'll be comfortable here... as long as this bungalow is in my possession. Who knows where you'll see me next time?"

We hugged each other again.

"All the best for your interview. We'll leave as well. It is almost evening, and it is an hour-long walk to the resort."

"Yeah, that Money Monk thing you mentioned. I would also have joined you guys, but right now, my priorities in life are different, as you can see. A job is the first thing I need to focus on."

"Yeah, of course. Please pass on our wishes to Ananya and tell her that we'll always stand by you guys, whatever happens. You guys are not alone. Trust us."

We hugged again, and Varun and I left the house.

We went back through the parking lot, and our smaller car shone much brighter than earlier. In just a couple of hours or so, our perspectives had changed drastically. We exited the gate and started to walk to the resort. As we silently walked through a deserted pathway through the fields, we could not help but relive the trauma that Kishore was currently going through.

"And we thought our lives were in a mess. Listening to Kishore's story is a revelation. I don't know how he will ever get out of the fix he is in," said Varun.

"True, I really don't know what will happen to our family if I lose my job today..."

"Yeah, we never think about the fact that we are immensely dependent on our jobs. Kishore's ordeal has brought back that realisation."

"Very true, but his is a different story. Yes, it will continue to occupy our mind space, but at the end of the day, it doesn't change our own lives. I don't even know how to get out of my own self-created mess. I mean, I want financial freedom, but it just seems too far. Sometimes, and especially after listening to Kishore, I feel that I should move to a smaller city or a village like this..." I said, pointing towards a few farmers still in their fields, winding up their daily business.

I kept venting at Varun as we kept pace through the pathway, "We will need to spend less, have a less stressed life, less pollution, and more happiness."

"Yeah, but farming may seem to be stress-free compared to our lives, but I am sure this is also not an easy life. We need to be in the shoes of the farmers to be aware of the challenges they go through every day," remarked Varun.

"True, I agree. The grass always seems greener on the other side. But it may not be easy for these farmers because they are dependent on their farming income and are therefore compelled to work – even if they don't like it, even if they are not well. They don't have a choice. But what if they had to do this as a hobby or passion? I am sure the experience would be entirely different."

"Okay, I get your point. Farming as a part-time option can be great. So tell me what stops you from making the move?"

"Not sure, Varun. I mean, where will the kids study? What will happen to Kritika's job? I mean, nothing is easy. We are a family, and it is not just about me anymore. Life has moved on. I have responsibilities to fulfil, and I may not be able to do that if I were to stay here, I guess."

"Yeah, it's just about the same with a lot of us, including me. We need to get financially free while staying put. I have no solution. Let us see if Money Monk has one."

"I am not sure exactly how Money Monk is going to help us. I enrolled for this programme, but we can't reverse any of these things – kids' education, inflation, work pressure – I hope he doesn't want us to become monks and shun our working life like he himself has."

We laughed and chatted as we walked to the resort. We have had these discussions many times earlier as well, but they'd end up in naught. If we tried to earn more, we would create more stress for ourselves, we'd invite more diseases, sacrifice our personal time and despite all that, our savings wouldn't change much. And Kishore's incident had further raised apprehensions about living a good life by earning more money.

"Yeah, true. I didn't even get an increment last year; my promotion was also due. But it's just getting tougher with every passing day. Sometimes I wonder, when life is so tough for us after having such well-paying jobs, what would it be like for most people who are not as fortunate as we are?"

"Maybe they are happier than we, like the farmer. They may be content."

"Maybe. On the other hand, there are people who are so filthy rich. Is there a problem with how we look at life? I mean, how do people get rich and financially free? I just don't understand how much they earn to get rich, really rich. I mean, not like Kishore, where you are earning well, but are so dependent on that income that you cannot survive without it. It is about freedom from the need to earn money – that is what I am truly looking for. But I have absolutely no clue how I'm ever going to get there, if at all," Varun sounded as dejected as I was.

"I think only businessmen can get rich. For someone with a job like ours, I do not think that there is any way," I remarked hopelessly.

"We will see, buddy. Let us hurry now. We will wait and see what this programme does for us. I have heard it is a mindset-changing one," confirmed Varun.

"Yeah, I have had similar feedback. So, I admit I am excited and looking forward to it. We need to move faster, I think. The Monk doesn't give any grace time, I've heard."

We paced up a bit. The fields were now left way behind. We were on to barren lands, with big rocks and muddy pathways. It would not take me long to repent my decision of walking barefoot. Our mobiles still had good connectivity, so we were able to pace ourselves well.

"But tell me, Manish, do you know why the Monk does what he is doing? This guy doesn't charge us much... I mean, the minimal fees he has charged will surely be spent on food and accommodation for the next five days, right?"

"Yeah, Varun, I heard he works for a non-profit. He just recovers the cost of conducting and managing this five-day workshop. I'm not sure if he is super rich or if he is an actual monk. It's confusing."

"Even if he is super rich, why is he doing this?" questioned Varun.

"No idea buddy, let us go and find out for ourselves. By the way, what is your daughter doing nowadays, Varun?" I changed the topic as we got closer to the resort.

"She is just finishing her eighth standard. She is already stressed about her studies, career, and other things. I remember how stress-free we were when we were her age. Sneha and I try to keep calming her down, but both of us are already so busy in our own lives that we are unable to spend a lot of time with her. And we regret that," sighed Varun.

"Yeah, true. Things are changing faster than ever before. Children nowadays are under social pressure, pressure from school, their peers and whatnot. It's tough for them. They're not as carefree as we were."

"Can't agree more, buddy!"

We kept walking through the terrain, guided by Google Maps. It was not long before we saw a cluster of huts.

"There, that must be the resort," I told Varun, pointing at them.

"Yeah... that must be it."

After a while, Varun shouted, "Here... here you can see the signboard... We must go right from here."

And we finally arrived at the Monks' resort, it was a truly divine feeling. In front of us was the main hut and the other huts were right behind. On the left was an area where some cows were being fed. It was closer to an *ashram* than a resort, and far from what we had imagined.

"The first surprise..." I told Varun as I pointed towards the cows.

He smiled back, still gazing at the place.

As we approached the main hut, we were greeted at the reception with lemon water. A lady in her forties named Sulekha introduced herself, forwarded a register and asked us to enter our details, including the unique registration number for the programme. Tall and smart, she had a cheerful demeanour and welcomed every participant with a smile and handshake.

We completed the registration formalities and wandered around the main hut. More participants were joining slowly. It was late in the evening by then and the sun was about to set. The lamps were already burning, emanating a sweet fragrance.

There was a provision for LED lights as well, but they weren't being used at the moment. I think they wanted to keep the area as natural as possible, and use modern means only for emergencies.

"Okay, we are just waiting for a couple of participants who will be here shortly. We still have thirty minutes to go. You can all make yourself comfortable and we will soon be meeting the Money Monk." Sulekha kept us up to date.

"Thanks, Sulekha," I acknowledged.

Sulekha was sweet, calm, and polite. We explored the area, but there was nothing much to do. The connectivity in our phones was present but weak. I sent a message to Kritika about my safe arrival at the resort.

"Please deposit your mobile phones here," said Sulekha, pointing towards an empty basket.

We obeyed like good students. One of the participants was sending a quick text – probably to his family – before depositing his phone.

"Okay, no smart watches, no other electronic gadgets. No watches, please. Deposit everything in this basket."

"Not even watches?" I whispered to Varun.

We all obeyed, though we didn't know how we were going to get up the next morning, without our phones or watches. We are so dependent on our gadgets nowadays.

"I am already so exhausted – that long drive, then that hefty lunch at Kishore, followed by his energy-sapping experience, not to forget the one-hour walk while carrying our backpacks. I am not going to get up before eleven tomorrow morning," whispered Varun back to me.

Soon the remaining participants had arrived, and we were all set to meet the one and only Money Monk. Our excitement and curiosity kept our fatigue at bay.

"Okay, all done?" asked Sulekha to confirm if the last set of participants had done their registrations."

"Yes..." they chorused.

"Great, then come along with me. Make sure that we don't chatter or make unnecessary noise. We will now walk down to the Monk's hut and meet him there."

We followed Sulekha. She walked out from the back door of the main reception hut and then traversed through a zig zag, but well-laid out path towards her destination. It was lush green on both sides of the path. We could hear the birds chirping, and the smell of the air was refreshing. After a couple of minutes, she stopped and asked us to wait outside a much smaller hut.

"Just stay here. I will seek his permission and come back. No noise, please. Thank you all for your cooperation," instructed

Sulekha as she knocked on the door and then marched inside the Monk's hut.

After a while, she was back.

"We can go in after about two minutes. Please make a queue as you go in. No noise. As you get in and meet the Monk, step aside immediately and let the others meet him as well. If there are any other questions, you can ask me right now."

None of us had any, though I kept wondering whether this was a programme on wealth creation or life elevation. I mean, I had experienced such silence, and such divine atmosphere in a few places, but certainly not in relation to money or finance or freedom. Anyway, everyone seemed eager to meet the Monk.

"Okay, follow me," Sulekha told the first participant in the queue. I think he was Romesh. I had a quick chat with him at the reception hut.

And then we all followed Romesh in a queue. I was almost at the far end of the queue. Finally, it was my turn.

Monk? All my biases associated with this word was shattered in a flash. Here was a guy in blue faded jeans and a while polo shirt. He was in his seventies for sure. Semi-bald and clean shaven, he had beaming smile as we all shook hands with him turn by turn.

We introduced ourselves but he asked more about each one of us. What did we do, where were we from, and so on.

The Monk's hut seemed ordinary, to say the least. Forget about any fancy stuff, there were no curtains, fans, or any gadgets.

The Monk himself seemed humble and down to earth with a face radiating joy, and soft hands, bending in respect while shaking hands with us. We were used to working with our supervisors in a corporate job and we had our own opinions about how a master should be like. But then, that is why he was a monk and not a boss – a Money Monk to be precise.

"Welcome you all to this session... I am happy to have you all here." He beamed at us as we finished the introduction session. We stood forming a semi-circle in front of him, so that he could address and see each one of us.

"Our pleasure, sir..." Most of us responded with utmost respect. I was not an exception.

We usually admire people who are highly skilled in some domain, but respect is a different animal. Respect flows out seamlessly only for the one who is highly skilled and humble at the same time. For example, I admired my supervisor for his domain knowledge, but I was never so humble and respectful, though he had a direct influence on how much money I made from my job.

"You don't have to address me with titles like 'sir', you can call me Money Monk, or the Monk, or MM, whatever you feel like. Just don't call me sir. None of us is inferior or superior to the others. We are all made by the same and made the same."

"So nice of you sir, but you are more knowledgeable than us. And probably that is why I respect you," I finally gathered enough courage to say something.

"What's your name, my friend?"

"Sir... oh sorry, Monk, my name is Manish."

"So, Manish, are you saying that you will respect me less if I did not have the knowledge?"

I paused. I don't think I had the answer. The Monk smiled, and his eyes rolled onto Varun, who was standing adjacent to me.

"What do you think? What's your name?" he said and shook hands with Varun.

"I don't think we will respect you any less," responded Varun.

"But why not? One of your batch mates just said that he respects me because of my knowledge," asked the Monk while referring to my response.

"I'm not sure, sir!"

"Sir?"

"Sorry, not sure, Monk," Varun corrected himself, as we all smiled.

"It's not what you know. It's not what you give. It's not what you have. It's how you treat others that earns respect. How you make others feel – it is the only thing that is perpetual, is remembered long after you are gone. Everything else is just so futile and transitional," explained the Monk.

He looked at Varun, and then at me with an ever-smiling face. We also smiled back in respect and admiration.

So, here we were, with a true Monk. He knew about life and understood humanity. But why were we here? We were not here for life skills. How would these skills solve our money problems in life? Anyways, now that we were there, we were excited to see how the programme would unfold.

While he continued to greet others and have short discussions, Sulekha intervened.

"Okay, I think it's time for all of us to leave. The Monk loves talking, and he can continue to do so till late at night."

"Oh, we thought monks love to meditate more and talk less," responded one of the participants.

"That is true. He also loves to meditate. But when he gets an opportunity like this, he relishes it. Anyways, we have other important things to focus on before the session starts tomorrow. Let us go, guys."

Sulekha showed us out, and we followed her instructions after saying goodbye to the Monk.

We were soon back at the reception hut, where Sulekha handed over a backpack for each one of us.

"What's this for?" asked Varun, referring to the backpack.

"I will just let you know."

"Doesn't he get bored, alone in that small hut?" I asked Sulekha.

"No, he doesn't have time to get bored," mentioned Sulekha.

I wonder what keeps him busy the entire day. No job and seemingly no family, I thought to myself.

"Yeah. At this moment, the Monk has gone for his meditation. He will see you all during the morning walk at six o'clock sharp in the morning," instructed Sulekha.

"But we do not have our watches or mobiles. How are we expected to be ready on time?" inquired one of the participants. It was a valid point.

"Don't worry about that," she tried to brush aside a seemingly genuine concern.

"No, but this is a valid question for most of us, Sulekha. We are used to waking up with an alarm. It is such a pleasant and soothing atmosphere here. It is so peaceful and so pollution-free. Everything is so relaxing. And to top it off, most of us are already so tired. I do not think that we can get up before noon tomorrow," I supported the other participant. Others nodded in agreement.

"Don't worry. You will wake up. I am telling you this based on my prior experience with the previous sessions and participants," reconfirmed Sulekha with a smile before continuing.

"Okay everyone. Please note that each of you has been handed a backpack which has important stuff for you like your badge, a step counter, water bottle, your hut number, and guidelines to be followed while being in the hut. You are all supposed to use this stuff and return the bag before you leave," instructed Sulekha.

"This may be a stupid question, but if you permit and if we have time, can I ask one question, please?" Varun asked Sulekha.

"Sure."

"This is a wealth creation programme, right?" Varun did not hesitate to ask what was probably going through everyone's mind.

"Ha ha ha..." Sulekha let out a big laugh, and each one of us was relieved that this question had been finally put across.

"Yes of course dear, what makes you think it is not?" she counter-questioned as she tried to control her laughter.

"I mean, I can't see meeting rooms, projectors, etc. We are not used to this. I mean, won't we be crunching numbers, analysing stuff, etc?"

"Don't worry. To achieve unique things, you must do them in a unique fashion," Sulekha's comments were reassuring.

"By the way, all of you must be hungry by now. Your dinner is served at the Hillside – the lawn behind the Monk's hut. You can look at the hut number assigned to each one of you. The details are in your bags. You can go to your respective huts, rest, and freshen up. I will be joining you all for dinner. You can follow the same path we followed to the Monk's hut and just go behind that hut. No noise please, as the Monk is meditating. If there are any questions, you are free to ask them."

"Well, yeah. Can we discuss tomorrow's schedule over dinner?"

"Sure, let us catch up then in an hour's time."

We looked at our hut numbers and started to disperse. Varun and I had got adjacent huts. So, we went about exploring together. Mine was #11 and his was #12. It didn't take us long to locate our huts.

"Okay, let us freshen up and meet directly for dinner?" I asked Varun.

"Works with me, Manish... see you there!"

***

By the time we reached the Hillside, it was already bustling with noise and energy. Everyone was chit chatting and getting to know each other. Of course, that was the right thing to do. We were there for five days. Knowing each other a bit more was going to help us.

More importantly, most of us had the common vision of saving more money and getting to financial freedom faster.

As discussions progressed in smaller groups of two to three participants, there were a lot of interesting insights we got from each other during dinner. We tried to understand each other's goals and dreams, our families, and what brought us to join the programme.

Sulekha was a part of our group now, and she was part of most conversations, giving us an insight to the programme. There was one couple among the participants as well. I really liked the fact that they came together. If nothing else, they would spend some quality time together. In all, there were twelve of us. A few of them had flown in from different cities in India, and one even from the US.

We proceeded to have dinner which consisted of healthy and wholesome dishes. We wolfed down our food in no time as all of us were rather hungry and exhausted.

"Okay, guys. It's late. We have an early start. We will get to know each other more during our activities tomorrow," announced Sulekha after we finished our meal.

"Will the Monk be joining us tomorrow? We missed him at dinner today," remarked Kavita, one of the participants.

"Yeah, he wasn't well today, but he will be there tomorrow."

"And what is the plan for tomorrow? What are we supposed to do?"

"You guys have a herculean task."

"What is it?"

"Get up early and go for a walk on the beach with the Monk," responded Sulekha with a smile.

"Early means?"

"6:30 a.m."

"It is truly herculean... and it is not going to happen," remarked Varun, shaking his head.

"It will... it surely will. See you guys. We will all meet here at 6:30 sharp. Be ready with your step counter band, and also remember to carry enough water. It is getting hot."

"How will we know it is 6:30 a.m.?" asked Kritika.

"You don't worry and trust nature. Just tell nature to wake you up at 6:00 a.m. so that you can be here on time," remarked Sulekha.

She was very confident that we would be there on time, and I was even more confident that there was no way we were going to reassemble so early.

***

I remember reaching the hut and falling on my bed straightaway. It had been a long, eventful day, and I was exhausted. When I opened my eyes next, I was surprised to hear the melodious chirping of birds outside the hut. It was still dark, though. I was not sure of the time, but I guessed it wasn't 6:00 a.m. yet. I tried to take another nap, but just couldn't. Nature was so inviting, and the birds kept calling. After a few minutes of restlessly tossing and turning, I got up and sat on the chair close to the window and looked outside. It was scenic, calm and peaceful.

I kept sitting there for a while with my eyes closed. Was I meditating? I had no idea. My eyes were closed, and I was engrossed in the sounds and fragrance of nature. Our posh but closed bedrooms never get the pleasure of watching the rise of the gigantic sun or hearing the morning chirping of these melodious creatures. Nature is beautiful. Waking up in its lap is a blessing indeed.

As the day started to shed darkness, I decided to freshen up. By the time I was ready, it was bright outside, enough for me to venture out and see if there were any others like me.

However, as I walked to the dining area, to my surprise, I realised I was among the last ones to reach there.

"Oh, you guys are already here?"

"I told you to trust nature. See..." Sulekha welcomed everyone with a smile.

"Yes, you were right, Sulekha. But I didn't get my belongings as you mentioned."

"Go, get them. The Monk should be coming here in ten minutes. By the time we hope that all of us will be ready to kickstart our day and our session."

Day 1

WHAT GETS IN IS ALL THAT MATTERS

"All set, team? Are your step counters ready? Water and fruits?" asked the Monk, brimming with energy.

"Yes..." responded some of us.

"Okay then, switch on your step counters, and follow me. Here we go!"

We all started walking behind him, as his brisk march made the dead leaves crackle under his feet. He didn't look like he was in his seventies. But then, the programme was full of surprises. He was full of energy. He was wearing running shoes, bermudas, a perfectly fitting blue polo shirt, and his step counter. He had a white beard that was nicely trimmed. He was partially bald, but his face had a perennial glow.

We walked through the jungle without much talking. We were just struggling to get used to the pace of the Monk's walk. Within no time, we could hear the sound of splashing waves coming from a distance.

As we started walking along the beach, we could see the sunrise on the distant horizon. The beach was calm and serene. Our walk automatically slowed down to allow the natural beauty to sink in.

"Okay, team, the purpose of day one is to set a strong platform for you. And there is no better place to set a strong foundation than this beach," explained the Monk.

He kept talking about the natural beauty around, and how it had helped him stay in shape for so many years despite all the diseases he had.

"I would have died a painful death, probably a few decades earlier, considering how many diseases I have been blessed with since the age of forty. But for my decision to quit my job and do something more meaningful in my life, I would not have gone so far. That strong desire to make my life more meaningful brought me here. And this has been a pure blessing."

We kept walking beside him – half of us on either side. His voice was loud and clear. The calmness of the beach allowed us to clearly understand what he was trying to convey.

"You don't seem like you ever suffered from any disease... you look so fit," I commented.

"I am still fighting them, one after another. But that's okay. That's life. I am happy with whatever *He* has blessed me with."

I kept thinking, He counts his diseases as blessings. He has a glow on his face and is leading a meaningful life. Why doesn't he have any regrets in his life, like the rest of us do? Of course, I didn't ask him this. It was the first day, and we were not familiar enough. But he had impressed us the previous day, and he won my heart this morning.

"Okay, guys, this session is not about me. It is about you. So, I have a few questions for all of you. Of course, the questions will have no fixed or correct answers. I am a part of you all. We are all expected to deliberate the questions among ourselves, and we will try to come to a conclusive answer by the time we break for refreshing coconut water – that's around 4,000 steps from here. Is that clear?" The Monk was precise and very clear in his communication.

We all nodded.

"Okay, great. Here we go. Why are you here?"

We all looked at each other. Courtesy to the previous night's dinner, most of us knew why we were there. We all wanted money, albeit for different reasons in life, but we were all there because we wanted to get rich and create significant wealth in our lives. This was a common denominator answer, and Romesh said exactly that.

"We want to make money, get rich, get wealthy and lead a better life," Romesh tried to be as precise as the Monk.

"Everyone agrees?" the Monk asked. Most of us nodded our heads in unison as we walked along.

"So, you want to make good money. Fine. Agreed. But are you guys saying that you are not making good money at present?" the Monk asked.

This was the first question where some of us had a difference of opinion, and we could clearly see that the Monk was trying to encourage different opinions and open us up for discussions.

"I feel that we are making good money, but probably we need to make more of it," said Arnab, a tall clean-shaven guy who, as I remember, worked for one of the best consulting companies in the US. He was an NRI and had come to India to meet his relatives and to attend this programme.

"Well, I think we are making good money," came another voice. I didn't remember this respondent's name.

"But we want to make more..." mentioned Varun, and I was inclined more to Varun's point of view than anyone else's so far.

The Monk picked up Varun's response and asked, "What will happen when you make more money?"

"We will get rich, and that is what we want," responded Varun.

"But why haven't you got rich so far?"

I wondered how he knew whether we were rich or not. And before I went deeper into my thoughts, he himself responded.

"And well, if you are thinking how I know that you guys are not rich enough, isn't that the reason you are in this programme? You are looking for something more, no?"

"Does he read our minds as well?" I whispered to Varun.

None of us had a clear answer. This question disturbed us. The cruel fact was that most of us were earning very good money. Someone like Arnab who has been earning in US dollars for almost two decades was still not rich. If that was the case, then what were our chances, earning in Indian rupees?

And then my thoughts went back to Kishore, our most successful friend. He was almost bankrupt after two decades of earning so well. Then how the hell were our lives going to be different even if we started earning more?

I kept thinking on those lines, and I'm sure the Monk guessed our uneasiness from the looks on our faces. He came over.

"Okay, relax. Are you guys confused?"

"I think yes," responded Varun.

"Then congratulations. Confusion is always good."

All of us looked at him in surprise. Everyone had a strange frown on their faces before he clarified.

"Confusion tells us that our mind is getting ready to learn something new," replied the Monk.

He continued, "Let me share some data with you. Person A makes ₹ 50,000 a month and Person B makes ₹ 80,000 a month. Who is wealthier of the two?"

Some of us thought that the answer was crystal clear. But I felt that it could not be so simple if the Monk was asking the question.

"Okay guys, we are almost done with 2000 steps. Another 2000 steps to go before our first refreshment break. Enjoy this beauty as long and as deeply as you possibly can."

The Monk picked up a shell that was swept to the shore and went a bit ahead and sent it back to the ocean – to its natural habitat where it originally belonged. He loved nature, and nature loved him back. It was evident on his face.

"So, who becomes richer? Person A or B?" he reinstated the question.

Some did say that Person A, for the obvious reason that the person was earning more. But I always loved to be a contrarian.

"It depends!" I shouted.

"There you go! Manish, right?"

"Yes, Monk," I reconfirmed my identity. He had a good memory as well. We had met him only once the previous evening, and that too for a few minutes, yet he remembered most of our names.

"Good, so it depends on what, Manish?" he asked.

"It depends on what we do with the money we made," I responded.

"Excellent!" he complimented me. And I felt like a school kid being praised by my class teacher, and relishing my bragging rights.

The Monk continued, "So, the money you make is important, but it is not the only thing that makes you rich. So, what is the other factor that can make you rich?"

"The money we keep," I responded. I had learnt this from my dad, but I do not think that I ever implemented this in my life. In fact, I didn't know how to implement it. I had the knowledge, but I never had the realisation of how powerful the statement could actually be. Kishore had made more money than we could ever imagine, but he didn't keep anything.

"Bang on! The money we keep. It's the money we keep that becomes our asset eventually, and not the money we make."

"But then the money we keep will depend on the money we make, no?"

"It does, but not much."

"How? I mean if we make two times the money, we can save two times the money, no?" asked Harry, the guy with the French beard in our group.

"Harry, what you say is obviously theoretically correct. But real life works differently."

"How?" was Harry's obvious next question.

"You see, Harry, the money you keep depends more on your dream, your reason for wealth creation and less on the money you make. Person A makes ₹ 50,000 and saves ₹ 20,000, while Person B makes ₹ 80,000 and saves only ₹ 10,000. Obviously, Person A will end up far richer than Person B."

"Yeah, true, but what makes Person A save more in spite of making less money?" asked Harry.

There was pin-drop silence. We were all waiting for the Monk to reveal some insights, but our mind was trying to go deep into the art of saving money. All we could hear were the tiny waves from the ocean singing their own beautiful song. And among these silent waves came the loud message.

"It is his purpose of getting rich, the strength of his dream, that allows him to save more and invest more. And thus get rich."

Our step counter showed that we were done with around 3,000 steps, and there was pin-drop silence again. Was the Monk saying that we all were focused on the wrong parameter all this while? Should we stop focusing on earning more? I never tracked my expenses or actual savings. In fact, I never ever took them so seriously. I don't know how much was being spent or saved. But was that really an important parameter? How much could that really help? I mean, I always knew that we could do a bit more to save here and there, but that could not surely decide how wealthy we got. Or could it? I had more questions than answers. His first few questions had already triggered a storm in my mind; a storm which was ceasing to wane.

"There... do you see that shade?" the Monk pointed towards a shaded area that was still some distance away.

"We will rest there, and I will treat you all with some refreshing coconut water. Just in case you have any questions, we can surely deliberate further."

We were all tired by the time we reached the shade. There was a stack of coconuts neatly laid on the table. We picked up our coconuts from the table and took a well-deserved refreshing break, not only physically refreshing but refreshing from the perspective of our minds; minds that had got rotten with just one way of thinking. We were questioning ourselves and our age-old beliefs, and I believed that was good. Not that I was fully convinced by what the Monk said, but at least there was someone who was trying to show us a different path. We had tried our own ways in life for so many decades now, and the results were not satisfying, to say the least. There was no harm in taking this advice seriously.

"Where's your coconut?" I asked the Monk.

"I won't have it now. I will have lunch straightaway," he responded.

"Don't you feel hungry?"

"Who doesn't, but I have got used to it. Intermittent fasting is a habit now. It helps me stay fit and keep diseases at bay."

"But don't you get the urge to eat?"

"Of course I do."

"Then, how do you control that urge?"

"My belief is that if the mind is truly convinced that the reason is strong enough, then the body can adapt to anything – virtually anything. The body can not only adapt, but it can also stretch, overstretch and rebuild itself. It can craft and transform itself into something that is totally non-existent today. The only condition is that your mind needs to be absolutely and totally convinced. Once that conviction is there, then it is all about having the patience and letting the body transform itself. And this includes the idea of saving more, and its impact on your overall wealth!"

I smiled, but my mind was stunned, yet again, hearing what the Monk just said. While he started chatting with the others, I never felt this strong internally. Our body can adapt to anything provided our mind is absolutely convinced. I couldn't hold myself long enough.

"You were talking about the strength of the dream that makes people save more... what exactly do you mean by that?" I asked the Monk, interjecting his chat with the other participants.

I think the Monk heard what I said, though he didn't react immediately. He kept looking at the farthest possible end of the sea, with his eyes probably tearing beyond that horizon.

He said the words that most of us will never forgive for the rest of our lives: "If the dream is big enough, facts do not count."

He continued, "The fact is that you are not saving enough. But if you have a strong dream, you can start saving more from today itself."

"But Monk, how much impact would this really have in our lives? I mean, how rich can anyone get just by saving more? And won't it impact the quality of our lives?" asked Romesh. Most of us had this question crisscrossing our minds.

"It has all the impact. In fact, it is the only thing that has an impact; otherwise, you will always continue to be what you are – Person B – earning well, but still struggling in life. It is not what you earn that makes you rich. It is what you save and invest that frees you from slavery and gives you enough to lead life on your own terms."

"I would love to hear more from you when you say this."

"Okay, Romesh, open up now. How much do you earn today?"

"Around three lakhs per month."

"And how much do you save approximately?"

"Around 50,000 per month, I think."

"So, what percentage of your income is your savings? Around 20 per cent, right?"

"Yes... correct," confirmed Romesh.

"And this is probably true for most of you here. And most people who still do not understand the importance of saving share the same statistics. They all save around 20 per cent of what they earn."

And I could not agree more. I was not even saving 20 per cent, though I wasn't sure. I had never actually tracked my savings so closely to be able to say what percentage I was saving.

The Monk continued, "Now, let us try to change how we look at this equation. Instead of looking at how much of your earnings you save, let us look at it from a different perspective, Romesh."

"Okay..."

"So, tell me now, your earnings are how many times your savings?"

We all got thinking. What was he trying to do... my engineering mind was running full throttle now. And I won the battle.

"We are earning five times our savings," I was the first one to respond.

"Yes, great! You guys are so intelligent. If you are saving 20 per cent of your income, we can safely say that you are earning five times your savings, right?"

"That is right, Monk, but what does that tell us?"

"That tells us that if you save ₹ 1000 more, you are effectively earning ₹ 5,000 more."

Monk paused. And we also didn't want him to proceed before we had gathered the crux.

As I got up to throw the empty coconut in the designated basket, I walked ahead a bit, away from the group, and closer to the waves. I kept staring at the sea and thought about the ongoing discussion.

If I could save an extra ₹ 10,000 a month, it is like earning an extra ₹ 50,000 a month. I did not know whether I could save this, but I had been working so hard for the promotion for so many years, and this promotion would not have led to an increment of more than ₹ 50,000 a month by any means. And I have been stressed, overworked and even doing things which were against my values – just for that one promotion worth an extra ₹ 50,000.

There was no guarantee whether I'd get the promotion this year as well. And even if I got it, what would it bring along with the extra money? More work and more stress. Was this acceptable? Was it good for me?

I hadn't looked at the expense side ever. What if there was a way to reduce the expenses by just ₹ 10,000, without taking any stress or pressure? Not sure if that was possible, but it was surely worth a try. It would make my life simpler, less stressful and more enjoyable.

I started to walk back towards the group as they were laughing and chatting. Someone must have cracked a joke, I thought.

"Okay guys, we are now going to walk back to our huts through the mini forest before the sun becomes too harsh for most of you. We will then assemble for lunch and continue our discussion there. Each one on your own now. No money discussions during the walk back. Enjoy the nature around you and let all this beauty sink in."

The group started to scatter and re-group in mini groups. Varun and I walked back along the path with the beach on one side, and coconut trees on the other side. We did not say a single word about money but we could not appreciate the beauty of nature as much as we would have liked to. Our minds were elsewhere.

“Bloody, all this while, we were focused on the wrong side of the equation,” I just blurted out. Varun smiled and agreed.

We reached the venue before we could break our chain of thoughts. Everyone started moving towards their own huts.

“Okay, catch you at lunch, buddy...” I told Varun as we made our way towards our respective huts.

I freshened up and sat on the only chair in the hut. In front of me was a neatly laid out table with some handmade candles spreading their natural aroma through the hut. Strangely, they had no electric bulbs in the huts. But what was even more surprising was a set of cards on the table. These were almost double the size of visiting cards. I just glanced at one of those, and it was titled ‘What makes you rich?’ The rest of the card was blank. I didn’t understand what I was supposed to do with it, and the other cards that lay there.

I was not very sure what time of the day it was so, I decided to walk down to the dining area where we were greeted by Sulekha.

“Mr Monk might be a bit delayed. You guys can start with your lunch. He will join you soon,” announced Sulekha to all the participants who had assembled.

We were all hungry and didn’t waste much time and started with a bang. Lunch was simple and delicious. More than that, it was very refreshing.

During lunch, the Monk also arrived. He was breaking his intermittent fast. This guy has some willpower, I thought to myself. But then I remembered his statement about a human body being all capable once the mind is convinced. But how to convince the mind. That was something we all lacked.

"How do you convince your mind and generate such willpower to eat after a break of sixteen hours – and keep doing this every single day?" I asked him.

"You can convince your mind only by a deep understanding of the situation. If you fear the situation, you will never want to go deep into it. But if you accept the situation, that fear gets nullified, and you are ready to cut through it and go deep. Only then will you find strong reasons to convince your mind. And once your mind is convinced, your body just obeys. Your mind is the master. Your body is just its servant."

Sometimes I wondered whether we were there for a financial session or a life session. It seemed a mix of both. Both finance and life have a deep correlation. Whatever it was, I was loving every moment of it so far.

"Can you enlighten us with an example?" My curiosity knew no bounds, irrespective of the topic of conversation.

"Asking 'why' holds the key. 'Why' intermittent fasting is important to understand. Similarly, 'why' should you focus on expenses, rather than income, is important to understand."

"Why should we focus on expenses? I think we know this by now. Because managing expenses will make us richer rather than focusing on income."

"That's right, but you need to go even deeper if you want to get passionate about saving more or spending less," replied the Monk.

"Deeper? Like?" I asked. This was getting interesting.

"Okay, let me ask you a few questions. Between the two – income or expenses – what is that you will deal with for a greater number of years in life?"

We were all grouped in a circle now, listening carefully to this Monk, who in the middle of this jungle, was briefing some of the most successful corporate executives about money. Wow!

"I think expenses," claimed Arnab, the NRI guy.

"Correct, Arnab. Your income is going to stop one day, isn't it? Whether you become financially free or not, whether you retire at sixty or not, there will come a time in your life when your body will not be capable of earning any more. It will either lose its skill or its physical ability to work. It may not happen suddenly. It may happen slowly. But it will happen, right?"

We all nodded in perfect symphony.

But what about your expenses? Will they ever stop?"

A big 'no' was our response.

"Correct. Never, not until you die. Forget stopping; your expenses will not even lessen at any stage of life. They will, in fact, just keep shooting up. Even after your death, your family has to spend quite a bit to perform your last rites. So, whether you have an income or not, you have no choice but to deal with expenses until your last breath. So, it is extremely important to start dealing with them right now and start getting deeper into your expenses."

We were all spellbound.

"Let us get even deeper. What will keep going up for sure – income or expenses?"

We all knew the answer but waited for the Monk to elaborate.

"Is there any assurance that your income will keep going up every month or every year? But what about expenses? Can you stop them from going up? Can you stop inflation?"

Those who were eating so far stopped eating in case their chewing sounds made them miss even a single word of wisdom.

"So, you are all dealing with a gigantic animal called 'Expenses' – something that never stops, something that keeps increasing in a compounded manner with inflation, and by the time you hang up your boots, this animal has become so mammoth that you are actually too late to be able to tame it. But here is the problem.

The problem is that you won't realise the animal that expenses are until your active income stops. When you stop earning, which you will surely do one day, and must dig into your savings to fund your inflated expenses, you will see all your calculations going for a toss and panic setting in. At that time, it'll be too late to earn more. You will just not have the energy, willpower or willingness to earn more. So, imagine a life at the age of seventy and you start to realise that you have no pension, you have no active income, your expenses are going up exponentially with inflation, and you have no energy to work anymore. How miserable can that life be? And there are a lot of people who are going to lead that miserable life – financially dependent on others, compromising on their health or small things that make them happy, excuse me..."

And Mr Monk paused to grab his plate of lunch and break his fast. We had all forgotten about our food by then.

We were all looking at each other's faces. We were the top executives from India and outside, ultra successful in our careers, and this Monk was telling us why we had been wrong so far. Crap. I couldn't believe how stupid I was, not sure what the others thought.

And the Monk returned after a few minutes with his plate full and eating, while we were all trying to come to terms with what was said. "While I eat, you can continue the discussion," said the Monk.

While the Monk savoured his neatly arranged plate full of vegetables, we discussed the topic among ourselves for the next few minutes.

When the Monk was almost done, we were ready to pounce with our questions.

"I think you have a point. We have not thought through expenses as seriously as we would now. I mean it is so tough to believe even now that we have been doing it all wrong."

"No, no, you guys are not wrong. Income is also important. Without income, there will be no savings. But the fact is that you are already focused on income. The challenge here is that you are focused only on your income. It's just that you are ignoring another key element of the equation – expenses. You are thinking it is not that important, or probably there isn't anything that you can do about it. That is where the problem lies, and that is where I want to help you."

"Yeah?"

"Just look at your parents. Do you think they generally did well financially, in spite of a very limited income?"

"Yes, for sure. Considering that income-earning potential was so limited during their time, they did extremely well to get all of us educated in the best possible schools and colleges."

"How did they do it?" asked the Monk.

"Because they were focused equally on managing their expenses as well. I get it," I responded.

"Absolutely. We lost that art somewhere in between when our incomes exploded. They saved and saved and saved and got rich – so rich that probably they have more net worth than many of you today, even if you have a hundred times the income they had."

"Interesting... and very true," I agreed.

"Mr Monk, you say that saving money is an art?" I questioned further.

"Yes, saving money is an art, because it is all in the mind. A mathematical formula just doesn't work. We know the mathematics of saving money. But it doesn't work at all. It is a mind game."

"How?"

"Well, let's leave that for dinner time. You guys enjoy your lunch now. Sulekha will guide you about the learning cards. You must fill them out before we meet tomorrow morning. You start filling them once you go back. The lessons you have learnt are what you want to take away from here. Catch you in the evening. We will check your physical strength when we meet."

Money Monk retired for an afternoon nap and left us surprised, as always. Now, why did he need to check our physical strengths? What does that have to do with money? And how was he going to test that? And why was a septuagenarian even talking about physical strength? We always had more questions than answers. Probably, that is what learning was. We never learnt the right way in our education system, which consisted of rote learning. This was how learning should be. We would discuss, deliberate, have opinions, and then we'd have more questions than what we started with.

"Okay team, you will find four learning cards on your tables when you go back," interrupted our wonderful host Sulekha.

She continued, "You can fill them now or after dinner as well. But do fill them. They are your takeaways from here. We are going to reassemble at around 5 p.m."

Sulekha read our faces and continued, "I know you don't have watches – so let me tell you all that you have about two hours. You can take a nap or just move around this tiny jungle. Don't worry, there are no dangerous animals out there. You can find a variety of birds, though. Also, your backpack has a torch and a first aid kit – just in case you did not check."

Sulekha laid the rules carefully and clearly. She was so calm, seemed well educated and very fluent in English.

"Any questions?" she asked.

I couldn't resist, "The Monk talked about testing our physical strength. So, I just wanted to know whether I need to be prepared."

Everyone smiled, as the same thing must have been running through their minds as well.

"You will find two watering cans – five litres each – at your doorstep outside the huts. In the next couple of hours, you must fill them with water and bring them when you assemble here for the evening walk," clarified Sulekha.

"Are you saying we are going to walk with a 10 kg load?"

"Yes, please."

"But why?"

"That the Monk will tell you. But train your mind so that your body can help you handle it well."

We were not prepared for this. There was so much that we didn't know. Was lifting weights also an art? Hopefully, we'd know a lot more by the time we left the programme.

All of us headed to our huts. It was hot as the afternoon sun was at its peak. But inspite of the hot weather, we never felt the need for ACs or even fans. In our workplace, which was not very far from there, there was no way we could survive without an AC. We were in a strange place. Was it a mind game? Could the body adapt easily and so quickly, when the mind was stronger?

As soon as I entered the hut, I threw myself on the bedding that was neatly laid on one side. There was a breeze blowing across the cross-ventilated windows in the hut. It may not have taken more than a few minutes for me to doze off. I don't think I ever slept so deeply so quickly. When someone can fall asleep without having the energy to make their bed, it is said that the day has been successful. And that day had been a very successful one indeed.

***

I woke up with Varun banging on my door and shouting at the top of his voice.

"Manish... wake up! We are late... I overslept as well. Get up!"

I woke up hurriedly, just combed my hair and started walking towards the assembly area.

"Hey bro... not that easy, man. Go pick up your cans," Varun reminded me.

I had forgotten about them completely. I saw two water-filled cans right in front of my hut and picked them up. Varun was already carrying his cans. We walked towards the assembly area. All the other participants seemed to have reached. The Monk was also there.

"Okay great. The two latecomers are also here..." said the Monk and smiled, clapping to welcome us.

"Ha ha... don't worry, we are not going to punish you further. You seem like you have already been punished with these two cans. Let's go, guys. You guys can follow me, and I will keep instructing you on the way."

We didn't get a chance to ask any questions. He walked with long strides, and also with his two cans. We couldn't complain. At half his age, how could we complain of not having the strength to carry what he was carrying with such ease and nonchalance?

We were just trying to catch up with the Monk as he traversed his way through the jungle to neatly laid out trees, big and small. It wasn't far away from the resort. Luckily, it wasn't an uphill path, but even then, the cans seemed heavier than ever before.

"Just a couple more minutes before we give you some relief," the Monk shouted from the front, as if he were reading our minds. He seemed to be leading and motivating an army contingent to move on and destroy the enemy.

"Okay, guys, halt here."

We stopped at an area where the jungle almost came to an end. But this was not the beach side of the jungle; it was the other unexplored side.

"From here on, you need to reassemble yourself into two groups – one group walking on my left and one on my right. On both sides, you will see small plants which need watering every few days. So, you are going to do a good deed today as you water these saplings. With the cans that you are holding, each of you should be able to water around ten plants. So, twelve of you plus me – thirteen of us should water a hundred and thirty plants today. We can go turn by turn – one person starts watering. As he or she finishes his water, he can give way to the other person. I will be the last one."

We were absorbing the rules when the Monk started to explain.

"We are expanding this jungle. The entire jungle that you have seen so far was created from rocky land, tree by tree. I started it, but then I alone couldn't have done much. It was only because of young and energetic participants like you that we have been able to expand this green cover."

We were lost for words. Was there anything this guy couldn't do? I couldn't hold myself and asked, "But why are you doing this? Do you love trees?"

"I am doing this to save lives."

"Whose life is at risk?"

The Monk stared at me and said, "Humans are not the only species on this planet. They are just one in more than a million."

"So, you planted all these trees?" asked Harry.

"Not alone. I could not have achieved this much without support from noble souls like you all. I am just trying to save the hummingbird through these forests. I hope I can, though I don't think I will be able to. But I must end on the correct side of history."

"But why are you concerned about a single bird? Why do you need to save one species?"

"More than ten thousand species go extinct because of the greed of one. Doesn't this bother all of you guys as to how we are systematically destroying nature, something on which our own survival depends? Doesn't this absolute stupidity from the most intelligent species bother you?"

We were all stunned and obviously had no response. This was the first time I saw him emotionally disturbed.

"Will this much water be enough for the next few days for a plant?" asked Varun.

"Yes, because it is the same personal finance principle of income and savings that gets applied in nature."

We had started expecting surprises by now. So, they were not really shocking. But I truly wondered what watering a plant had to do with saving money.

"Don't be confused. I will explain it to you during our dinner conversations. C'mon, guys, the faster you water, the earlier you get rid of the load that you are carrying."

We all began. The ladies were given the first chance. And then we all followed. It must have taken around half an hour for all of us to finish the task. And all the while, the Monk described each tree we were watering – the variety of the tree, its history, significance for the human species, etc. He explained how trees talk to each other, help each other, signal each other and how they also experienced feelings like most humans do.

We had never thought so much about trees our entire lives, and none of us had ever met someone with such in-depth knowledge about trees.

"Okay, if we are all done, we can start walking back with our empty cans."

We obeyed him. While walking back, we observed each tree on our way back through the jungle, and pondered about how they must have been nurtured and grown into what they were today. It must be such a fulfilling experience for the Monk.

"They are my extended family – the only one I have now."

"Only one? May we ask about your family members?" asked Kavita.

"They are no more. The family perished in a flash... just one accident."

"Oh, I'm really sorry," she responded.

"No, why should you be sorry about this? Wasn't your fault, right, unless you were the one driving the truck that took them away from me?" he laughed.

The respect we had for him increased manifold with every single conversation.

***

We arrived at the assembly area soon. It was sunset, and oil lanterns were being lit. Sulekha was finishing off the last touches before dinner.

"Dinner should be served in fifteen minutes," informed Sulekha.

"Okay, guys, while we wait for dinner to be served, we can open this forum for any discussion," said the Monk.

The Monk was in a mood to talk that day, and we were happy to grab the opportunity.

"While watering the plants, you talked about how the idea of watering is the same as saving money. I have not understood that," started Kulwant.

"Ah, yes, see it is not difficult to understand. I told you that we need to go deeper to understand the problem. That strengthens and convinces our mind. Remember?"

"Yes, yes..."

"So, you can go deeper by studying the subject – personal finance in this case, or you can also look at another way to convince your mind, and that is by observing the world around you – nature, fellow humans, studying human history, etc."

We were listening and absorbing.

"See, it is simple. How do you think we get energy in our body, Kulwant?"

"By eating food and drinking water. I mean, what I know is that the cells absorb the energy from the food we eat, store it, and use it. That's all I know."

"Right, so is it what you eat that matters or is it what gets absorbed by the cells that matters?"

"But if we don't eat..."

"I am not saying you are not eating. You are eating, but is eating alone good enough, if your body cannot absorb what you eat?"

"Both are important."

"Exactly, Kulwant. And where are we focused?"

"Only on eating."

"Right, can you correlate eating with your income and absorption with your savings? At the end of the day, if your body cannot absorb anything, you are a dead man – eat whatever you may. You are also dead if you don't eat."

"I get your point. It's the same concept. If we do not save anything, we can never get rich, irrespective of whatever we earn."

"Right, and the same thing is seen in other parts of nature as well, like watering the plants. You can water as much as you want, but if the soil cannot absorb it and pass it on to the roots, or if the water just gets wasted or evaporates in sunshine, then there is no way the plant can survive or thrive. It doesn't matter what you bring in; what matters is what is taken in."

We all stumbled. We were getting the crux of getting wealthy. The amount of money we brought in didn't matter. It was the amount that got saved and invested that mattered. If the money was not being invested, then there was no point earning whatever one might be doing so.

"Here..." the Monk handed over an empty water bottle to Haider.

"Hold this bottle for me – straight up," he instructed and Haider obeyed. This bottle was labelled as 'Wealth'.

"Here... hold this," the Monk gave me a water bottle similar to mine. And this one was full, and was labelled as 'Income'

"Now, it's very simple, but when we exemplify this, the lesson will be etched in your minds. And the more it gets into our minds, the easier it is to implement in our lives. Now, Manish is going to pour some water from his 'Income' bottle into the currently empty 'Wealth' bottle that Haider is holding. Let us see how much Haider can take over for you guys. Start... It's a simple exercise."

Haider was about to open the cap of his water bottle when he was stopped.

"No. You are not allowed to open the cap," clarified the Monk.

We were all perplexed. What was the Monk expecting – that the water would go into the other empty bottle by magic?

"I know you guys are perplexed. But that's what it is. Start..."

I knew the outcome, but I had to start anyway. So I did start trying to pour the water into Haider's closed bottle slowly, and expectedly the water spilled over. We looked at the Monk but he didn't react.

"Okay, so now that you guys aren't able to do this simple task, let me help you by making a small hole in the cap."

The Monk looked towards Sulekha, and she obliged like a professional. She replaced the original cap with the one that had a small hole.

"Okay. Go on, Manish."

I knew I had a chance now and tried to very carefully pour the water into the empty bottle. A lot was still getting spilled over. But there was a tiny amount getting in for sure.

"What do you observe? And don't tell me that water was not going in earlier, and some water is going in now. That everyone can see. But what's your observation in the context of your income and savings?"

We were all quick to grasp it now.

"Our income is useless if all of it gets spent, and we don't save anything to create wealth."

"Excellent. What else?"

"It's the savings that fills up the other bottle, and not the income. What gets in is what matters. The bigger the savings or the hole in the cap, the larger the wealth creation."

"You guys are very smart and need to be rewarded with dinner immediately."

We all smiled.

As we started to get up for dinner, the Monk shared another perspective of life and savings that would reverberate with us for a long time that night.

He said, "It's the same everywhere, folks. I can keep giving you all the knowledge in the world, but that is all useless. What matters is how much you take in. So, what is going to change your life is you, and not me. I am important. Rather, I am potentially important. But what is going to enrich you is only what you take in."

Dinner time was absorption and reflection time, rather than active discussion time.

"You talked about saving money as art, and not science," Haider began.

"Yes, that's the crux of the programme over the next few days. I am going to show you techniques to strengthen your mind and tame your expenses. Without that, it is almost impossible to control your expenses, and they will always creep up to match your income."

"Interesting. Can expenses be controlled with the mind? I mean it sounds ridiculous, but for example, how do I control my grocery expenses by controlling my mind?"

"Yes, you very well can. Everyone can. In fact, there is no way you can control your expenses unless you are able to tame your mind," the Monk replied.

We all looked at each other.

"Are you saying that we start eating less and do intermittent fasting like you? I cannot do that," Haider said, shaking his head animatedly.

And we all burst out in laughter.

Smiles, laughter, fresh air, good food, clean water, and good company – what else did a human want? I was starting to fall in love with the place. Perhaps the mind was being prepared for the art of saving money and getting rich. As usual, dinner was warm, delicious, and filling. The Monk bid goodbye as soon as he was done. He probably went to sleep early or meditated at bedtime.

"Okay, team, this has been a great day. The Monk is very happy about it. He asked me to convey his thanks to all of you. You are free now. You can do whatever you wish to do until you are off to sleep. Please remember to turn off the lanterns in your huts before you go to bed. Oil is precious. We don't want to waste it. Also, as I explained earlier, you'll find the learning cards on your table. They are relevant for today's learning. Make sure that you fill those out. It will help with the absorption of the learning and will serve as a reminder for you when you leave this programme. And you now know how important it is to absorb?" smiled Sulekha.

We all smiled. We understood very clearly by now that all this knowledge being showered here would be useless if we did not absorb it.

"Any other questions?" As always, Sulekha was crisp, clear and to the point.

"Not much, except that what's the schedule tomorrow?"

The schedule remains the same every day. So, we all get up at around six in the morning with the help of your biological clock. The rest, you will get to know tomorrow.

"Okay."

"Good night then, team! See you tomorrow," Sulekha bid goodbye to all of us and headed towards her hut.

We strolled back to our huts. Varun and I sat together in my hut with my learning cards. We needed to do this homework before hitting the sack. Anyway, there was nothing else to do – no TV, social media, IPL, political news, entertainment, music, magazines or newspapers. How could the Monk live like this every single day? The Monk perhaps had the capability of being a monk, but how did his staff, people like Sulekha and all the other support staff survive?

"Buddy, we have four cards for today... should we do it together?" asked Varun.

"I think that we should do it independently, though we can sit together while we do it. Everything is personalised here. My learning can be slightly different from yours."

"I agree."

We started on our homework. It didn't take me much time, though. Things were getting crystal clear.

Here were my four cards for the first day:

Day 1
What gets in is all that matters

WHAT MAKES YOU RICH?

It's not our income, but our savings and investments that make us rich.

Learning Card#1

Day 1
What gets in is all that matters

WHAT TWO FACTORS INFLUENCE SAVING MONEY?

Income and Expenses are both important in helping us save money.

Learning Card#2

Day 1
What gets in is all that matters

WHAT FACTOR IS IGNORED WHEN SAVING MONEY?

All our emphasis is on earning more income. Expense Management is usually ignored.

Learning Card#3

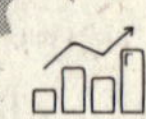

Day 1
What gets in is all that matters

IS SAVING MONEY A SCIENCE?

Saving money is a mind game. It is an art. We can save more if we can strengthen our mind.

Learning Card#4

Day 2

RESIST THE HERD

"I think I overslept," I said to myself as I looked at the bright sunshine outside. I got up quickly and had a good bath. Soon after, I rushed to the breakfast lawn. I was right. I was late, very late.

"Here he is, finally..." said one of the participants.

Everyone began clapping while I wished the earth would swallow me up.

"No, you don't need to feel embarrassed. It will happen to all of them. You guys are not used to waking up with your biological clock. It takes some time to set that up before it is activated. Just pick up that takeaway breakfast for you. It will be a bit dry, but that is the best we can offer you without wasting everyone's time. But the fruits are quite juicy," said Sulekha, as she pointed towards the packet prepared especially for me.

I picked up my breakfast packet humbly.

"Okay, we are assembling at the old neem tree opposite hut #9 in the next ten minutes. The Monk will be there waiting for us. I will let him know. And remember that today there's a trek on the cards. So, take the trekking stick and wear your trekking shoes on the way to the starting point. Of course, you need to carry your backpacks as well. No trash to be thrown along the trek. Everything must go into the backpack. Follow the directions that the Monk will show you. I will also be following you guys as I love trekking. Any questions?"

We didn't have much to ask. Everything was so well planned. We rushed back to our rooms for our backpacks and trekking shoes. Most of the guys in the corporate world were used to this last-minute rush. We reached the old neem tree, making sure we didn't take longer than ten minutes.

"Good morning, folks, just follow me for the next ten minutes for the right direction, and then the trek itself will guide you," instructed the Monk as he kick-started our day's trek with his usual brisk walk. Sulekha followed him, and all of us trailed behind Sulekha.

The trek wasn't that steep, to be honest, but it was steep enough for city dwellers like us. We were huffing and puffing very soon, though we were glad that we were in a pollution-free environment and doing something good for our body and mind. It had been more than 36 hours, and we hadn't yet looked at our mobiles or laptops. And it felt good. We had more energy for sure – much more than we thought.

The wild flora and fauna on the way were amazing. The chirping of birds, and the buzzing of strange insects, along with the fresh breeze was mesmerising. It had been a while since we were in the very midst of nature. Even during our vacations, we stayed in hotels with their usual manicured lawns and had our meals at the buffet. This was refreshingly different.

And my views were about to be challenged.

"Okay, team, it is a ten-minute uphill climb now. We should be at our destination soon. We will meet some fellow travellers there. Get... set... go..."

"The Monk is too disciplined, man. Was he in the army or what?" I asked Varun.

"Don't know, buddy. And wonder who we are going to meet at the top?"

"No idea... he keeps surprising us."

We were sweating within a minute of the uphill climb. Our water bottles in the backpack came to our rescue. The bag also had a packet of salt solution in the first aid kit, in case we felt dehydrated. I didn't feel the need for the time being.

We managed to reach the top, and threw ourselves on the patch of nature's green carpet. While we were still breathing heavily, what we saw in front of us was shocking, at least for me. I looked at the other participants. Most were drinking water, their eyes pinned on what lay in front of them.

There was a small plateau among the hills – something very rare to find. But it was not the land formation that surprised us. It was none other than the Monk.

And what was he doing? He was feeding and cajoling four horses. We a were shocked to see other animals as well. There were sheep, dogs, chickens, cats, rabbits – I mean was this the Monk's farm or zoo?

"Meet Vasco," the Monk said, urging all of us to come closer and feel the strongly built horse. We obeyed without a single word being said. I had never touched a horse in my entire life so far.

"Vasco is a Portuguese breed, originally bred for war. This breed is highly sensitive, incredibly intelligent, surprisingly beautiful to watch in action, and a joy to be with."

We could see the joy on the Monk's face as he kept cajoling Vasco as if he was his family member. I think the key to Monk's fitness was his closeness to nature – be it trees, animals or birds.

"Do you guys know that horses are flight animals?"

"What is a flight animal by the way?" I asked.

"Good question. A flight animal is one whose natural reaction to any situation in which it feels threatened or uncomfortable is to run away from the situation. And do you know where they run to?"

"Where?"

"It is always to the herd to which they will run. To their mind, there is always a lion waiting just out of sight that wants to eat them, always."

We were all already in awe of the Monk's knowledge, but this one took up the admiration a few notches higher. Not that we had any doubt about his financial wisdom, but this was a different level.

"But do you know how a horse gets bred for war when it is always chasing a herd?" Monk continued.

We were all silent, showing our damn ignorance of the world around us.

"It has to be trained intensely to ignore their most basic impulse of following the safety of the herd, and instead stand on the ground and face up the threat in front of them. This requires years and years of rigorous and patient training. And the training will succeed only if the horse trusts the rider, puts all his faith in him that the rider will protect him, and not let him be harmed by that imaginary lion."

"Wow, interesting."

"But why am I telling you all this?" asked the Monk.

There was pin-drop silence, yet again.

"I am telling you all this because this is true not only for Vasco, but also for the other horses. This natural feeling of safety in the herd is true for most animals, including us humans."

"There you see... it's so beautiful," the Monk pointed towards the sky in a specific direction, and we all looked up.

"Isn't it beautiful?" asked the Monk.

All of us nodded our heads as we stared at a clear blue sky. "Yes, really, it is blue and clear."

"But there was nothing extraordinary in what you just saw. You just followed the herd mentality. Many people are saying that the view up in the sky is beautiful, because I am saying it, and thus it must be true. This is your natural tendency. And there is nothing wrong with such a tendency. It comes naturally to all animals. And so, you'll tend to have it as well."

We didn't know whether to appreciate the Monk's wisdom or feel embarrassed about our own ignorance. But it didn't matter. We were there to learn.

"So, are you saying that herd mentality is natural? We always thought it was negative," remarked Harry.

"Herd behaviour is natural. It is inbuilt in humans for a particular reason, and as you just saw, the prime reason is safety. Many animals naturally live and travel together in groups called herds. Goats, sheep, and llamas, for instance, live in herds even today, as a form of protection. They move from one fertile grassland to another without any organised direction."

By this time, it seemed that we had trekked to the top of this hill to watch a National Geographic channel shooting happening live in front of the animals with the Monk being the commentator and host.

"For safety reasons, they become one large, big unit, though each one of them is an individual. So, this tendency to group together is a safety mechanism. But the herd is good only when safety is needed. The same tendency to follow the herd becomes one of your biggest wealth destroyers when there is no need for herd-based safety."

This guy is crazy. How did he just observe and connect money to nature?

"How do you even make these connections, Monk?" I just couldn't stop myself.

"Because everything is a part of nature, and everything obeys the laws of nature, and that includes you, and that includes money."

"But how can following the herd destroy our wealth?"

The Monk was patting the other animals while Sulekha was busy feeding some of them with her own hands, as we waited for the Monk to respond to my last question.

"Do you know what Black Friday is? Have you ever been to a Black Friday Sale?" responded Monk.

Though we had all heard about the Black Friday Sale, we all looked at Arnab since he had been in the US for a long time.

"Yes, I have been to one. Every year, during the Thanksgiving holiday and the subsequent weekend, Black Friday unleashes a frenzy of shopping. Retail stores and online sites offer massive discounts, and people rush to grab deals. I mean it is crazy... There are long queues outside Walmart stores, and people queue from three in the morning, six hours before the stores open. It's crazy to see such scenes in the US!"

"Right, this is the herd mentality kicking in as individuals follow the masses, hoping to snag bargains. The fear of missing out drives this behaviour, even if it means joining the chaotic shopping spree," commented the Monk.

"Okay, let me share another example. Imagine two nearly identical restaurants – one crowded and the other empty. Where would you prefer to go with your family?"

"The crowded one," I responded.

"Right, but why? What's the reason? You are just assuming that the crowd signifies better food. However, this choice might be based on coincidence rather than actual quality. But you can't help it. This is natural herd behaviour on display, and as we talked about, all animals display it without exception."

"Okay, but how exactly is understanding this herd mentality going to help us in terms of saving more and getting rich? I mean, I am still not clear."

"Of course, I don't expect you to be clear. We are going to talk about two interrelated concepts – Lifestyle Inflation and Induced Consumption – during our lunchtime discussions, and that will give you the context of what's happening inside our minds that is not allowing us to save much more than we are currently saving. As I said earlier, you need to understand what is happening inside your mind. Why are you thinking in a particular way, and then strengthening your mind to save more and then invest more and then get rich faster? Saving, as we discussed earlier, is an art, and not a science."

We cajoled some of the animals to come to us. The place was a perfect blend of flora and fauna. I wish we could have stayed there longer. The Monk had been truly doing something worthwhile with his life. He was creating things and protecting lives which would be cherished long after he and all of us were gone. It had been a serene experience so far, but now the Monk was hungry as he had been fasting for almost fifteen hours.

"We start the descent in ten minutes. You can enjoy the natural beauty till then. Vaishnav is here. He is the caretaker of all these animals in our absence. If you wish to ask anything about any of them, he is the expert."

The Monk never wasted even a single moment. He had ten minutes, and he immediately sat down to meditate. I wondered about his state of mind as he meditated. I was going to ask him some day. I wished to meditate and get deeper into spirituality too, but the hassles of a job... I don't know when I'd start working on my own dreams.

The descent was faster, though less exciting than the ascent. We headed to our huts, freshened up and went straight to the lunch area. As usual, we gathered our plates and were ready for a chat with the Monk.

"What do you think about when you meditate, even when you have a few moments to spare?" I just could not hold myself.

"I just close my eyes and chant while trying to visualise my deity. That's all about it. For me, the idea is to train my mind not to get distracted by unnecessary things, and for that, I need to train it to focus on one thing – who better than my deity. I just chant his name."

"Wow, that is interesting. How long are you able to chant at a stretch?"

"Not more than twenty seconds without distraction. I have been trying hard to increase my focus for many years now. I have improved, but the target has no upper limit, just like making money has no upper limit."

We all laughed again. He could connect anything to money.

"Okay, on a slightly serious note, and to keep the tempo moving, tell me the increase in your income in the last five years?" Monk asked an open question to the entire batch of participants.

"Mine doubled"

"Three times"

"Roughly two times...."

Everyone began sharing their numbers.

"What about your expenses during the same period?"

This time, the responses were fewer.

"I understand the lack of response. Many of you are not even aware of the increase in expenses, because you have never actually tracked them. But if any of you have been tracking them, can respond."

"Well, expenses have actually gone up more steeply. They have caught up with the increased income. I haven't actually tracked expenses very closely – but have a rough idea," responded Kulwant.

"That's fair! Many of you are not tracking your expenses. But you guys have a fair idea that expenses have caught up with your income. And that is a universal fact."

"What is a universal fact?" asked Chandra.

"The tendency of expenses to catch up with a higher income is a fact that applies everywhere."

We relished the food and the knowledge being imparted. Both were worthy of our time spent there.

"But why does this happen? Why do expenses go up with income?" Chandra was in no mood to give up the discussion.

"It's inflation, man," remarked Kulwant, who was one of the participants who rarely spoke. And of course, we all knew that inflation was a killer. We nodded in agreement.

"Yes, inflation, but do you think that regular inflation is so high that it can just double up your expenses in about five years?"

"It works in a compounding fashion," Kulwant replied.

"Yes, Kulwant, you are right. Inflation is for real, and it works in a compounded manner, but doubling your expenses in five years would mean a consistent year-on-year inflation of almost 16-17 per cent. Do you think that inflation is that high, actually? What are the government's published inflation figures?" inquired the Monk.

"Well, 6-7 per cent usually," responded Kulwant.

"Right, even if we assume the regular family inflation to be 10 per cent, then what happened to your expenses? Why did they rise to catch up with your increased income?"

We had no answer. So, we focused on the food instead. We looked at the Monk. He was expecting someone to come back with a counter argument or a question. He didn't enjoy preaching and always wanted a healthy discussion and a lot of questions.

He waited and waited until the bald-headed Chandra broke his silence yet again.

"Is that something to do with our herd mentality?"

"Bingo! Chandra, you nailed it. Yes, it is. But your mind needs more convincing than that. Just knowing that it is herd mentality will not bring in the desired result. And this is the right time for you all to understand the concept of Induced Consumption," said the Monk.

"What? Can consumption be induced? I mean, if I don't want to consume anything, how can someone induce it?" Chandra was in full flow.

"So, let me explain how Induced Consumption actually works and then we will know how to deal with it."

The Monk was also at his savage best, and we were loving where this conversation was going. It also made me wonder why couldn't our Indian education system be based on such meaningful conversations between teachers and students, rather than rote learning, strict set of topics, chapters and so on. Anyway, I had to stay focused on the Monk, Chandra and Kulwant.

"But I also heard of something called Lifestyle Inflation. What's that?" Chandra, our inflation expert, was in no mood to give up.

"Lifestyle Inflation is also a result of Induced Consumption. We will come to that, Chandra. You must first understand the concept of Induced Consumption, why it happens, and how it plays in our minds. Then, we will know its impact, and then we can think about controlling it. So, let us go step by step. Let me get some more curd... excuse me."

Mr Inflation, aka Chandra, followed him.

"Mr Inflation!" I shouted.

I had nicknamed him Mr Inflation and made it official by calling him out, as he glared back at me. He probably didn't like my nickname, but I was in no mood to give up so easily.

The Monk and Mr Inflation were back with their respective refills, and as he relished breaking his fast, he continued:

"Induced Consumption is consumption of regular goods and services that varies with income. As your income grows, so does your disposable income. As disposable income rises, so does the rate of Induced Consumption. When disposable income is zero, Induced Consumption is also zero. As your income grows, you tend to enjoy more lavish lifestyles, make additional purchases, and incur greater expenses. So, essentially, Induced Consumption responds to changes in income, allowing for more discretionary spending and investment. It's simple. Your income goes up, you don't have that many expenses, so you have more to save, but you won't save; rather, you start spending more."

"But why would we spend more? Why won't we save more?" asked Kulwant.

"Because you are also an animal," responded the Monk.

Everyone was stunned and relaxed when they saw the smile on the Monk's face.

"I mean, you would spend more because of the inherent pull of all animals, including humans, to follow the herd. That is your natural instinct. Look at the car you own today and the car you owned just five years back, when you had half the income. Look at your mobile phone, your clothes, or your shoes. With increased saving potential, you have tried to keep pace with the herd."

"I mean, that is so true. Even my watch, the restaurants we go to, the movies, everything has kept pace with our disposable income. We could have saved the extra and invested it to get richer. But we haven't," I agreed.

"But is that life? I mean, curbing our needs to get richer?" came the response from Harry.

"Well, I was waiting for such a question. This is a very broad and personalised question for everyone. The definition of life is different for everyone. I do not know whether curbing your desires to achieve something worthwhile is life for you or not, but I know for sure that this is not your need, Harry. This is over and above your need. This is greed; this is exactly what follows the herd in the modern world. Our herd feeling tells us that we cannot be left behind the herd. Your needs are food, shelter, security, and clothing. But the kind of clothing you can wear depends on your disposable income. You need a car. Yes, for sure, you need a decent, trouble-free car which can take care of your family's needs, but would a car priced at ten lakhs that is new, good quality, branded, spacious be good for your family, or a BMW worth sixty lakhs? How you bifurcate a need from the herd mentality is vital. But even more important is why should you bifurcate?"

"But would we be leading a happy life if we were left behind the herd?" I asked.

"Do you think I am leading an unhappy life?"

We all looked at each other and smiled.

"Of course not," I reaffirmed on everyone's behalf.

"When we are not in danger, then you do not need to follow the herd. You need to drop the herd mentality. You need to resist that inner urge which is trying to drive you towards the herd. In fact, staying away from the herd in normal times can fill your life with happiness and bliss."

"Are you saying that we will be happier if we don't chase the herd?" asked Harry.

"You got it absolutely correct, Harry."

Harry didn't seem convinced, and the Monk knew that.

"See Harry, staying away from the herd allows you to choose your own direction of life, rather than being led by the direction, or the lack of direction, of the herd. You can chase what you love doing. And chasing what you love doing is what is going to give you happiness. Otherwise, within a short span of time, a BMW or a Mercedes will keep you as unhappy as a basic model of a decent car."

"But couldn't a BMW be a dream for someone? Could it not be a passion for someone?"

"In rare cases, it could be. But in most cases, it's just herd behaviour. You must ask yourself why you are buying it. I mean, if you have too much money, and spending it on such a luxury doesn't impact your freedom or other important life goals, then there is no harm in going for it, though it won't give you any additional happiness. But be wary of the fact that such possessions have no upper limit. The upper bar is a continuously rising goal post and thus keeps you consistently unhappy in the absence of never having achieved that moving goal."

"I get that. This is interesting that moving goal posts always keep us unhappy, and the top of wealth is a moving goal post too." Harry was slowly getting convinced.

"Good that you have started absorbing the ideas. Let me give you a very simple demonstration of why following the herd is likely to keep you unhappy. Harry, come here..."

The Monk called Harry close to him, kept his lunch plate aside, and asked Harry to walk towards Sulekha.

"You have to walk from here to the point where Sulekha is currently standing. That must be around 100-120 metres. But you can only look upwards while walking."

"Upwards means? Towards the sky?"

"Yes, please," confirmed the Monk as he picked up his lunch plate.

Harry started walking. He was confident to start with, but he soon realised how tough it was. He almost tripped many times, but managed to totter to the point where Sulekha was.

"Great... now come back while looking in front or looking down," instructed the Monk.

Harry followed the instructions and reached his original position with ease and much quicker.

"So, which way was easier, less stressful and made you feel happy?"

"Obviously the way back."

"Right, so remember this all your life. Not only is the top a moving goal post, but you are more likely to trip if you keep moving ahead in life while you are looking at the top. Even if you do not make a trip, your journey is likely to be stressful and unhappy. He who looks down while walking life's journey is truly able to enjoy life."

Our body was absorbing the food, and our mind was absorbing the wisdom spewing out of the Monk's words. It was sheer brilliance of simplicity. There was nothing extraordinary about what he was saying, but the impact was enormous.

The Monk continued, "Good. Now, a car was an extreme example. You will not be buying a new car every day or every year. But Induced Consumption enters ever so silently into your life. It is the upgrade of smaller things like your clothes, gadgets, watches, and everything else that touches your life. This Induced Consumption, driven by your herd mentality, leads to what we call Lifestyle Inflation. You have upgraded your lifestyle, thus leading to increased expenses, and therefore, your expenses catch up with your income. At the end of the day, you don't save much and stay poor. Even staying poor with a lavish lifestyle is herd behaviour. There is a tendency to believe that a better lifestyle while staying asset poor is the right thing to do because the herd is doing the same."

We all absorbed this conversation silently. It was very enriching for each of us present there.

"So, that 16-17 per cent inflation was a result of 7-8 per cent general inflation and an equal amount of Lifestyle Inflation. You may not realise this, and you may keep blaming inflation for high expenses, but you won't even realise at what point you started following the herd. When you blame inflation, you are basically telling yourself that expenses are not in your control. But it is only when you realise that you have a massive component of Lifestyle Inflation, which is driven by Induced Consumption, that the onus to control expenses starts to fall on you. It is when the onus falls on you that your mind starts to get convinced that something can be, and should be, done to change the situation."

"This is interesting, but now that we know it, can we not tame the Induced Consumption?" asked Chandra.

"It's very tough to," replied the Monk.

"But why? When we have the knowledge, why is it tough to change?"

The Monk smiled as usual and responded.

"Ask a chain smoker why it is tough to give up smoking despite knowing that smoking is killing him. Ask a foodie why it is so tough to give up on uncontrolled gluttony despite suffering from obesity and other related diseases. Ask yourself why it is tough for you guys to go for a morning walk despite knowing the benefits that would accrue. The point is that knowledge doesn't change you as a person. Knowledge is obviously the first step, but you need much more than knowledge to bring in a lasting change. And if the change is related to how you are crafted as a species, like in the cases of getting pulled into herd behaviour, it's even tougher. You are all crafted to be associated with herd mentality. This mentality leads to Induced Consumption, which drives your Lifestyle Inflation. To break that herd is going to need something special."

"Then what is the point of studying all this if we cannot tame something as simple as Lifestyle Inflation?" Chandra sounded disappointed.

"Yes, you have a point. I am not saying that you cannot. All I am saying is that it is not easy, and just knowledge is not going to be enough. Of course, I will tell you how some people have been able to do it. If we can inculcate the same principles as successful people, we can do it as well."

We were all ears, but we were reaching the fag end of our lunch. And Sulekha was back with her carefully crafted instructions.

"We are taking a break now. The process remains the same with just one change. Try to make sure that you keep filling in the learning cards during every break. Your learning cards for today have been placed in your huts. This ensures enough mind-jogging so that you have the right questions ready for the evening meeting. Also, we are going to have a competition among all the participants in the evening, and the top rankers will be rewarded as well."

There was always something to look forward to. But before we departed for our huts, I made sure that I ate, and ate, and ate. The physical endurance of the morning trek had left us famished. And the aroma of the food had invigorated so much hunger that I forgot that I had learnt from the Japanese. Japanese centenarians from the Blue Zones (places where people live exceptionally longer) advise everyone to fill a maximum of only 80 per cent of our stomach. And that has proven to be one of the keys to a long and healthy life. I became a prime example of what the Monk had been saying. Knowledge and implementation are two different animals altogether. I couldn't help packing my stomach beyond its capacity. Knowledge is accessible everywhere in today's digitally connected world, but implementation needs strength of mind, and that is precisely where this species is at its weakest.

After overstuffing our stomachs, we headed back to our huts. And the next immediate challenge was right in front of me. I was facing a neat bed in front of me with my stomach full. But I had to resist my desire and fill up the learning cards before I hit the bed.

Sulekha's efficiency was on display yet again. The learning cards were neatly kept on the table with a note to fill them up as soon as we see them, and not to procrastinate.

I sat in the chair and started with my homework. As I pushed myself to write down the learning cards, I started to relive the day and enjoy the moments yet again. It's funny how our mind changes instantly – from a sleepy mode to a hyperactive one, just in a few seconds. Filling up the learning cards wasn't tough. The questions were simple, and the impact was spellbinding, so much so that I found it tough to sleep in spite of a tired body and a full stomach. I was now able to relate to Monk's words of wisdom. I was realising that it is not the body, but the mind, that decides when to sleep. So, if you can push your body beyond your comfort zone and work on an area that rejuvenates your mind, the body's need for rest or sleep will wane away in no time.

I had filled up the cards in no time.

Day 2
Resist the Herd

WHY DO WE FOLLOW THE HERD?

Following the herd is a natural mechanism in humans for a sense of safety in times of fear.

Learning Card#5

Day 2
Resist the Herd

IS IT GOOD TO FOLLOW THE HERD?

It is not healthy for individuals in normal times to follow the herd.

Learning Card#6

Day 2
Resist the Herd

HOW DO EXPENSES REACT TO HIGHER INCOME?

Expenses tend to catch up with increased income. This happens because of 'Family Inflation' and 'Lifestyle Inflation'

Learning Card#7

Day 2
Resist the Herd

WHAT KEEPS US UNHAPPY WHEN FOLLOWING THE HERD?

The top of the herd is a moving goalpost and gives us a feeling of having never been able to achieve our goal in spite of our best efforts.

Looking up, towards the herd, and moving forward in life is a stressful activity.

Learning Card#8

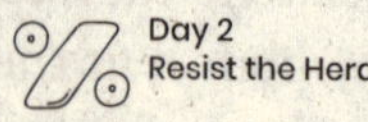

Day 2
Resist the Herd

WHICH MICRO-ECONOMIC THEORY DRIVES LIFESTYLE INFLATION?

Induced Consumption drives Lifestyle Inflation.

Induced Consumption is a result of 'increased income' and 'herd mentality'.

Learning Card#9

I felt very relaxed after filling out the learning cards. I was getting into the groove of the biggest secret of wealth creation – to save more. My mind was getting convinced to resist the herd, because that was the only sure shot way to happiness.

I was also realising that the biggest reason why we are not able to save more is because we do not understand the art of saving money. It is not about sacrifices or living a timid life. It is all about understanding the economic theories behind the art of saving money, and how we can strengthen our minds to break the template we have been unknowingly put into, ultimately leading to wealth creation.

These concepts were simple to understand, but I was also sure that the key lay in the implementation, and that is where it is going to be tough. But then so be it. I was determined I would adapt to it. I'd take on the challenge. It was about *my* freedom, and I understood very clearly that nothing worthwhile in life was going to come easy.

I threw myself on the bed, as if I had not slept for a long time. Within minutes, the expected happened. I was in a different world. When we close the open threads in an active mind, it shuts down immediately. And that was perhaps what the learning cards were doing. All our open threads were getting closed by revising the learnings of that half, and that was critical for the mind to shut down. Who could have understood this better than the Monk, and who could have implemented it better than Sulekha?

It was only Varun who brought me back to this world.

"Manish! Manish, get up, man. We are late... yet again!"

I don't know how many hours I slept, but it felt as though an entire lifetime had passed.

I didn't react to Varun. I smiled at him as if I had been born anew and there was no burden on my shoulders. I felt light, just like the bird outside the window.

"Oh, sorry man... just give me a few minutes. Relax. Have a seat. I will just freshen up quickly and come along," I tried to calm him down.

I was done in a few minutes and we headed to the lawn. There was an air of excitement among the participants who had already assembled there. The competition was about to start. We waited for the Monk to come over to the arena.

"Okay, all set for the competition?" the Monk tried to boost us with his energetic tone as he walked in.

"Yes!" shouted most of the people. I was still half asleep, but I did nod.

"Great! The first competition is a 450 m race."

Oh no... a race? And that too when I am half asleep? And we are not kids. We are all corporate executives working with the best of Fortune 500 companies, I said to myself very well knowing at the back of my mind that there would be a strong reason for any event in this resort. Nothing was a waste of time or effort.

But running immediately after waking up was not a brilliant idea. But then, I was a decent enough runner so decided to give it my all. Some participants gave up mentally even before attempting. But then, the competition was on.

The Monk started explaining the objective.

"You guys must run through the periphery of this resort, just like the runners do in a track race, and come back to this starting point. Of course, Sulekha will note down the timing for each of us. I will be the last competing participant – no. 13."

"Bloody what? This seventy-year-old guy is going to compete with us. It will be a shame if we lose to him. I just hope not," whispered Harry.

All of us overheard Harry talking to Varun. I think the Monk heard it as well, though he didn't care. In fact, he knew how to make the best out of naysayers.

"Yeah, it's not easy to beat this septuagenarian. I can challenge most of you," responded the Monk with a smile.

We shared a good laugh when Sulekha intervened.

"Okay, we will do a recce of the race track once with me. Though some markings have been made along the track, still it is important to avoid any confusion," she clarified.

We did what was asked and returned to the starting point.

Soon, we were all set to run, along with the Monk. We all began stretching to get ready for the race. The atmosphere was suddenly very competitive, reminding us yet again of our corporate world.

"Guys, all set? I will start the countdown, blow a whistle, and off you will go. I am your judge as well, so those starting the run before the whistle will be immediately disqualified. No excuses. No second chance. Is that clear?" Sulekha alerted.

"Clear!" came the chorus.

"Three... two... one.... Go..." Sulekha with a pen, paper and timer clock in her hand, blew the whistle.

And we all ran to the best of our abilities. We had to be careful while running since the track was not actually a racetrack, and none of us wanted to fall or get injured. I was puffing halfway through and had to slow down a bit. The Monk was way ahead of many, including me. He was in the third spot. My competitive spirit pushed me harder.

As we completed the track and reached the starting point, we gave our final push. Some of the participants were taking it very seriously and were running as if it were a do-or-die situation for them.

Sulekha, along with two colleagues, noted down the timings of each participant.

First rank went to Arnab with a timing of 81 seconds. And you know what, I was ranked third – not bad by any standard, considering that I had not run for ages. The bulky and bald Chandra, our Mr Inflation, came last. But then, he was glad that he finished the race. Everyone's definition of happiness is so different, I thought.

By now, you would have understood who got the second rank. Yes, it was the Monk. Not that he showed any emotions, but most of us could not have imagined at the beginning of the race, that we would lose to an old monk.

Sulekha presented a chocolate to Arnab as promised at the beginning of the race. She clarified that there were no other prizes for any other rank. Kulwant and Harry, who were relegated to the last few ranks in the race, raised an objection.

"I think it's not fair to judge someone based on just one skill," revolted Harry.

Kulwant nodded in agreement.

"Why?" asked the Monk, his face smiling now after catching up with his breath, as if he was happier with the question than the race itself.

"See, we are not good at running, but you are judging and rewarding us on the basis of a skill which is not our strength."

"Fair point, Harry and Kulwant. What's your strength?"

"I am good at singing," replied Kulwant.

"I am good at English communication," claimed Harry.

"Okay then, Sulekha, would you be kind enough to arrange a word-making competition while we have our evening tea."

I could sense a bit of stress on Harry's face. Was the Monk so good at English that he could beat our Harry? No one knew.

The Monk gave Sulekha some time while we sipped our tea and relished the home-made snacks. The food was always very energising. Don't know whether it was the impact of the weather or the Monk's effect or something else.

"We are all set," interrupted Sulekha.

We all participated in the word-building game, though it was not the strength of many of us. By the time we were close to the finish, we could see that Harry would get the top rank, followed by Arnab. He truly knew his strength. The Monk was relegated to the third spot this time. So, again, no prizes for anyone other than Harry.

"Should we have a singing competition now?" asked Monk.

"We don't mind," I mentioned, as Romesh came up with his objection.

"If that is the case, then I would recommend a badminton competition as well, if that is feasible."

The Monk and Sulekha smiled.

"I think we are expecting too much from Sulekha, though I get your point. It would be unfair if we did not have that competition."

"Yes," many agreed.

"So, we had two competitions so far, each one with a different winner. But you would have observed that each competition was marked with protests. What does that tell us?" the Monk addressed all of us.

"Each one has different strengths. A singer cannot win a race, and a runner cannot win an English competition." I volunteered to answer a rather simple question.

"Absolutely! Now, let us have another race..." said the Monk.

I wasn't very keen, but I didn't mind. I enjoyed my last run, and this would also give me an opportunity to beat my past score. And who knows, we might beat the Monk this time.

"But this time, we will not run independently," clarified the Monk. "This time we will run as a herd and see the results."

"Means what? How will that happen?" I was confused, and I'm sure all the others were as well.

"Sulekha will be tying our hands. So, my right hand will be tied to someone's left hand and his right hand to someone's left hand – thus we will form a chain or a herd, and then we'll run together."

It sounded strange. It took me back to my school days. We used to have many such funny races. But we only had fun and never learnt any lesson.

Sulekha asked us to stand in a queue, and she started tying our hands. We had now formed a chain, and no one could outrun the other partner. We were officially and formally a herd now.

Sulekha whistled to start the race.

It was fun to start the race, but chaos prevailed immediately. I was not able to run fast enough since I was tied to someone else. And the same with the Monk. Arnab, our last winner, fell trying to regain his last position by running too fast, not adapting to his herd partner. We all had to stop in between to pull him up, and then we started to run again. We pushed, pulled, scrambled, adjusted, and did our best to somehow finish the race. It was a painful run for most of us.

"No prizes for anyone," said the Monk as he pointed towards Sulekha to open the hand ties.

We all smiled.

"So, what did you guys learn?" asked the Monk as we all threw ourselves on the lawn, huffing, puffing while skirting the dirt from our clothes. We seemed far more exhausted than on the last run. Our timing was poor as well.

We were still catching our breath. And we really did not know if there was anything to learn from this chaotic experience. But the Monk was waiting for our response.

"I think it was a chaotic race. None of us enjoyed it!" Arnab was the first one to respond, probably disappointed about not getting his hand on another reward this time.

"Yes, brilliant, what else?"

"I mean, this was not even a race. I am sure we, as a team, took more time than the worst timing of our individual race," responded Haider.

"Excellent. Kudos to you guys. You learnt the lesson so well."

I was wondering what there was to learn before the Monk clarified.

"The first thing you must take note of is that when you are a part of the herd, you end up with poor results along with the entire herd. A herd does not even reach where you, as an individual, could have reached easily."

It sounded interesting.

The Monk continued, "Secondly, and even more importantly, you did not enjoy the journey when you were a part of the herd. This was because you were running a race which may not be your strong point. Your strength may not lie with the strength of the herd. We saw how I could not match Harry in the word-building competition, but Harry could not match Arnab in the first race. Our strengths are different, and it is almost impossible to match our strengths with those of the herd."

We were awed by the message that a simple and chaotic race could convey.

The Monk continued, and we were all ears.

"It is good to be in a herd when faced with a disaster, but generally in life, you must break away from the herd, check your strengths, and move in a direction that supports your strengths, else you will neither be good, nor will you enjoy the journey. We have already seen how a herd will always keep you unhappy, which matches none of your individual goals in life. Am I making sense to you guys?"

There was a momentary silence, and then we could hear Romesh's query.

"Does this breaking away from the herd to chase our goals and enjoy the journey have something to do with our financial savings as well?"

"Excellent question, Romesh. Yes, it certainly has."

We were all ears.

"Breaking away from the herd is the first way to break away from Induced Consumption. You don't need to run the race that everyone is running. You need to find your strength and run your own race. If everyone is buying a big car, gadget and the like, you don't have to. You should be driven, not by the herd, but by your goal. If your goal demands a good gadget, then yes, please go ahead and buy it, since it may actually aid your goal. But if your goal demands saving more money, then you are driven by that goal and need not follow the herd. Remember that when you are running your own race, you don't need to beat anyone or anything – you must look at your need, pursue that and enjoy the run. There is nothing more satisfying than running your own race and enjoying the run."

We were all in awe of the simplicity and clarity of what this old guy was telling us. I realised the importance of breaking away from the herd. I realised that if I did not break away from the herd and chart my own path, then neither could I meet my own goals in life, nor could I enjoy my life. I must craft my own life. It had nothing to do with the life of my neighbour, my colleague or my friend.

My train of thought was interrupted by Sulekha.

"Okay, guys, the food is ready. It's already past dinner time. You guys might want to freshen up."

We gathered for dinner and began plating our food. The Monks' words were reverberating in our minds, and we did not want to break their chain of thought.

"So, if I want to be a travel blogger, what do I do? I got your message, but I am unable to connect your message with my own life. Can you help?" asked Kavita, who had varied interests like cooking as well as travelling.

"Yes, and I wish to learn and teach yoga," mentioned Harry.

I also pitched in, "I want to write books."

"I want to practice organic farming," said Varun.

And the atmosphere was charged with everyone sharing their dreams and passions.

No one was quiet, and no one was feeling hungry. Our hunger was currently satiated by the genuine possibility of living our dreams.

"Okay, I get that. But what's stopping you from doing what you want to really do?" asked the Monk.

"Our financials. Our families are not yet secure. We don't have enough to cater to them for their lifespan, so we need to continue to earn. And my yoga sessions are not going to give me enough to keep feeding my family," mentioned Harry.

"Yes, but do you even have a plan to break yourself from the herd and follow the path of your choice?" said Monk.

"Can we ever?" countered Varun

"Yes, of course, you do not need unlimited money to achieve financial freedom, and then pursue what you wish to. You can plan to accumulate enough for your freedom, and then be ready to break from the herd and follow your dreams. Even to accumulate enough, you need to break yourself from the herd first. The herd will buy the latest car, but your freedom goal will demand that you break away from the herd and manage with a smaller and comfortable car. The herd will run after the latest gadget, but you must stick to your existing gadget if it is serving your purpose. The herd will keep running the maddening money race and keep shifting the goal post of how much they want to achieve in life, and stay stressed and unhappy. But you will have to put a cap on the money race, understand how much is enough for you and your family, achieve that, and then chase what you love so that you can live a life that is worthwhile and satisfying.

"This maddening money race has no upper cap. The herd will continue to run in this race for their life and will still find itself short of happiness and a sense of achievement, because by the time they reach one point, the goal post will have already shifted higher. There is a minimum amount of money you need to take care of yourself and your family. Get there, and then put on a cap and tell yourself that you decided to break from the herd because your strengths are different, and you want to enjoy this journey."

No one was eating now. Everyone was listening while holding their plates in their hands. No one got up. No one wanted to get up. We wanted to dive deeper into our dreams, get drenched in them and smell the aroma of how it feels to live a life of one's own dreams. We relished this until we were pushed to come out of reality.

"Okay, everyone, let's get on with dinner. The Monk can keep you engrossed through the night, but we must finish dinner quickly now," Sulekha jolted us out of our thoughts. She was a great time keeper as well.

There was a strange silence as we began eating. Hardly anyone was talking. It was probably for the first time that someone had shown us that we could be financially free just by saving some more money. And all we must do to save more is to break away from the herd. Financial Freedom would be that trigger point at which we could start to chase our true calling in life. We were still imagining a probable beautiful life, and were mentally elsewhere as we gobbled up the food.

By the time we were done, we realised that the Monk was already retired for the day. Sulekha was wrapping up along with the meagre staff available at her disposal. She worked so hard, making all the arrangements. She was the first one to arrive and the last to go, and I had yet to see any hint of tiredness on her face. I kept wondering how she was always so enthusiastic.

Now that the Monk had already gone, I went to chat with her. Varun also joined me.

"How come you are always cheerful and glowing?" I finally asked Sulekha.

She smiled.

"No, this is no flattery. We all see that," Varun reconfirmed my views.

"I really don't do anything special. It's just that I love this work and am happy. Probably, that's what gives me the glow."

"But you seem to be very educated, talented, fluent, and efficient. Why didn't you try for a job in the corporate world?"

"Because I broke away from the herd."

This one hit us hard. This last sentence from Sulekha summarised what Monk had been trying to teach us the entire day. Suddenly, there was a volley of questions. By this time, the rest of the participants had also assembled around her. And we were a chorus.

"This is so nice to hear," Harry said. "You are a living example of what we want to be. Knowing that we must break the herd, and meeting someone who has actually broken the herd are two different things altogether."

"Align them in ascending order, please," she instructed the staff to arrange all the utensils in ascending order of their size.

"You are so good. I know you broke the herd and are now doing something you love, but do you get paid much, if I may ask?" Harry was trying to get deep, though he also seemed a bit hesitant, just in case he was crossing the boundary.

"Sure, you can ask me anything. I don't get paid at all," Sulekha went straight to the point.

We looked at each other in surprise.

"Really? I mean, what motivates you in that case?" Varun continued.

"Money can never be a motivator beyond a point for anyone. The fact that I can contribute something to a group like yours is a good enough reason for me to work. I work for the mission of the Monk."

"Mission of the Monk? And what is that?"

"To help you guys reach freedom."

"But what is his interest in making us financially free? Why would anyone do that, especially considering that there is hardly any fee for this programme?"

"Because he has a larger purpose, which is to elevate our society. And he knows he alone cannot do much. So, he wants you to achieve freedom. He believes that most people are generally good, and when they are not constrained by the compulsion to earn money, they will certainly do good for society in their own special ways. See, his way to elevate the world around him is to plant trees. The entire jungle, you see, was planted and nurtured by him over the last fifteen years."

"So, does he expect that we will get freedom and help him plant trees?"

"No... he doesn't expect you to plant trees. He expects that God might just bless you with the wisdom to see that true happiness is always in giving, and you can find a way – a special way which is unique to you – to elevate the world around you. Some of you may teach, some may feed, some may open libraries. You would do whatever excites you. But he wants you to be enabled enough to start thinking on those lines. And your freedom is the enabler."

"But what if none of us do anything of this sort after getting freedom?"

"That doesn't happen."

I am unable to understand what you are trying to say.

"One day, each one of us gets the wisdom to understand the need to contribute to the world around us. For some, wisdom may come before freedom, for some after freedom, and for some very late in life. But as and when you get that wisdom, you should already be free by that time, so that your mission is not constrained by any compulsion to earn money."

"Wow... I feel blessed to be a part of this beautiful group. Had you not taken our mobiles, I would have created a WhatsApp group right away, and always stayed in touch."

We all had a good laugh. But down somewhere, we were realising the pettiness of what we were currently doing with our lives. It was time to return to our huts, fill the learning cards and then sleep over all the thoughts that we had garnered that day. It was a day well spent indeed.

"Thank you so much, Sulekha, for sharing all these insights. This sets an interesting perspective."

"You are always welcome, guys. Okay, so tomorrow, we have a walkathon in the first half. So, be ready in shirts and shorts. Rest, you already know by now," remarked Sulekha.

"Cool. See you then, Sulekha. Good night."

"Good night all of you."

***

Back in the hut, I was physically exhausted by the gruelling day, but mentally charged up with the revelations that we had been fortunate to be a part of. I sat excitedly on the table and did my best to fill up the learning cards.

Day 2
Resist the Herd

WHY IS IT IMPORTANT TO BREAK FREE FROM THE HERD?

My strength is not the same as that of the herd. To execute my strength, I need to break free.

I will never enjoy the journey if I travel with the herd.

Learning Card#**10**

Day 2
Resist the Herd

WHAT IS THE MEANS TO CHASE YOUR DREAMS?

Find your goal. Plan for your freedom.

Break from the herd. Save more.

Get to freedom quickly. Chase your passion.

Learning Card#**11**

The night was going to be long. There were so many dreams that I had put in cold storage. It was time to take them out, dust them off and start visualising them. I had to plan for my freedom, and for that, I had to break away from the herd. Breaking from the herd would allow me to save more, invest more and get rich faster.

I fell asleep that night. But life was waking up on me.

Day 3

MIRACLE OF SELF-MONITORING

It was just the third day, and we were already used to getting up without an alarm clock. Our biological clock was taking over, albeit biology included the chirping of birds in the absence of an alarm clock. The sun was about to come up.

Silence rarely sounded so soothing. No traffic honking, no milkman, no pings on the phone, no grocery delivery, no rush to reach anywhere. A human experience in the lap of nature should be natural and obvious, but has become so rare in our modern world. I was glad that I had been able to experience it again.

I was up early. I came out of the hut and took a deep and long energising breath. I looked at the trees around the hut. They were decently tall now, though they never ever gave the feeling of a real jungle. I understand that it would take time. Everything worthwhile in life takes time. To believe that the Monk had planted and nurtured each one of them with his own hands, with some support from participants like us, was amazing. He must be a really satisfied man to see the trees grow.

I felt the Monk was akin to a parent who watched their children grow up – all that nostalgia of them being kids, their tantrums, their adverse health situations, rushing for school, the fun games, the hugs, the disappointments, the stress – everything that was a part of growing up. I am sure each of these trees was just like a child for the Monk, each one defining their own story of the relationship between two of nature's most amazing creations – the humans and the trees.

Just like we were going to leave behind our children as our memories, he was going to leave behind the jungle for us, and for all those birds and insects that resided there.

I was still lost in my thoughts when Varun came and patted my back.

"C'mon, there is a bit of change in the programme. We must first go to water those trees along the trek, and then be back here in an hour."

"Oh, I didn't know that... sure, let's go."

I also wanted to give a bit to this jungle. Sulekha was right. The blissful feeling of selflessly giving something to nature, or to someone else, was a different experience altogether.

The Monk did not accompany us, but Sulekha did. We carried the cans and did our bit for the trees. It was a fast job and was the perfect warm up for the day's learning. It felt good, as always.

"Okay, thank you for a wonderful job done... a big clap for this team, everyone."

And we all clapped for ourselves. I was feeling like patting my back and saying to myself, "Wow, good job, Manish! At least a slice of your life was meaningful." I was just thanking God before I was interrupted again.

"Off you go for breakfast and reassemble at this point in thirty minutes. The Monk will join us. And eat well as there's some hard work ahead," tipped Sulekha.

After a most satisfying breakfast, we were all set – mentally as well as physically. And seeing the Monk was ever so refreshing.

"Good morning, Monk," was the chorus.

"Good morning, all of you. Hope you had a good time watering the plants."

"Yes..." we all shouted in tandem. The energy levels were up. In fact, they'd been rising since we came to the place.

"Okay, then, stand in queue, and Sulekha will help us divide this group into two teams."

We obeyed. It seemed as though a competition would be held once again. We were all set for some more learning.

"Okay, remember your number... 1,2,3,4,5..." Sulekha started counting one for each person in the line.

"All even numbers on my left, please; and all odd numbers, please move to my right," instructed Sulekha.

We obeyed.

"Okay, listen to me carefully now. The left side team will be led by me, and the right side team will be led by the Monk. Let us see which team wins."

And before we could ask her any questions, she clarified the rules.

"This is a walkathon competition, but with a difference. It is a team competition and not an individual one. Both teams will play this activity and formulate their own strategies to do their best and come out as winners. Each team is expected to complete a walk around the same track where you ran yesterday. But no one is allowed to run. You must only walk. The Monk and I will monitor that very carefully. The team that runs will be disqualified immediately. When you walk as a team, you must hold each other's hands and form a chain."

"Just like a herd?" Romesh piped up.

"Ha ha... yes. Just like a herd."

Sulekha continued, "Each team will complete ten rounds of walking on this 400 m track. The team with the fastest total time after adding the timing for all ten rounds will be declared the winners. Any questions?"

"Yes... What if the chain breaks by mistake during the walk, or someone trips, or if we take a break?"

"It should not happen, and that is why this is not a running event. You must just walk. But in any such case, you must restart that specific round from the start. So, for example, if my team's chain breaks somewhere during the fifth round, I will ask you guys to go back and restart Round 5 from the beginning. And I will be very strict about it."

"One more question."

"Yes, please."

"Will we get some refreshments in between?" asked Haider. He was worried about his hunger pangs. Haider was fond of eating, so his query sounded legitimate.

"Yes, that is your choice. We have enough earthen pots on the way. Oranges are available at this point. It's up to us, team leaders i.e., the Monk and I, along with the team to decide what strategy to adopt to improve our chances of winning with the best possible time. Clear?"

"Yes"

"Okay, one last thing. Each of the teams will initially get fifteen minutes before the start of the walkathon to frame a winning strategy for this competition. Any other questions?" asked Sulekha.

"No..." confirmed Haider.

"Okay then, all on my left – please stay here. I will be your leader. The ones on my right – please go and join your leader the Monk. It is around 9 a.m. right now. We will take fifteen minutes for strategising then we start this 400 x 10 walkathon – a four kilometre walk in total – and then we reassemble at the dining area for lunch. We will announce the winner there."

Everyone obeyed.

I was in Sulekha's team. Sulekha stepped away a little bit, faced all of us, and took all of us in a huddle. It was time to strategise for victory.

"So, guys, go on. What rules or strategies do you think we should adopt to win?"

"I think we should have fast walkers on the extreme right and left of the chain and relatively slow walkers in the middle. The fast ones can pull the weak ones," I was the first one to go with my suggestion.

"Okay, sounds good. And who are the fast walkers in our group?"

As we went about giving suggestions, Sulekha was prompt in documenting the worthy ones, so that we could shortlist them and decide. She exhibited all the skills of a great leader – patient, clear, decisive and a team player.

"I think that we should take a walking break, rather than break during our walk. We can eat or drink while walking."

"Yes, done... noted."

She went about her task of strategising in a very professional manner. And soon, we reached a conclusion, which was effectively imparted to all team members.

"Okay, so we've agreed to these three rules."

Sulekha read out the documented and finalised rules to her team. She made sure that everyone listened and understood them.

"Done? Shall we go?"

"Yes, we are ready."

"Okay good. This is a timer clock. It's quite big in size, and I will keep it here at the starting point. From a distance, each one of you will be able to see the time elapsed during every round. I will note the start time on my register. Then, I will walk with you and keep motivating and helping you during every round. Someone from our team needs to note the time taken for each round in this register kept here."

"But if we stop to note the time for each round, we will just delay our overall time," remarked Kavita, who was a part of our team.

"Yes, a little bit, maybe... but it is good to understand this data, Kavita."

"Do you really think so? Isn't our purpose to win rather than to analyse the data?"

"Yes, you are absolutely right. Our purpose is to win, and that is precisely why we must note this data," Sulekha said in an authoritative tone.

Now, this was tangential. Of course, so far, all competitions and activities had taught us important money lessons, and I was sure that this one was also aimed at that, but this truly sounded absurd to me. I mean how can spending time on noting down the data help us win a competition? Was Sulekha going too far, or were few more of our existing beliefs about to be shattered? Only time would tell.

"Okay, any other suggestions or questions, team?"

"No, we are all set."

"If during any of the walkathon rounds, if anyone needs any help, please call me out. I will be along with you. Don't break the chain else you have to restart the round... remember?"

"Yes, clear."

"And, if anyone trips or falls or anything, call for help."

"Done..."

"Aren't our rules too simple? I am sure the Monk'll have smarter rules," I was worrying about the competition.

"Well, Manish, I can't comment on that. Let us focus on what we have control over and do our best. At the end of the day, remember that winning is important, but not the most important thing. The pursuit of victory can help us enjoy the journey or make it a stressful experience. It is all up to us. Winning is never as important as enjoying the journey. So, c'mon team, while we will do all it takes to win, make sure that you make this walk the most unforgettable walk of your life. Enjoy it. Look around as well at nature's beauty. Breathe in and breathe out deeply. Take care of each other. Get to know each other. Help each other. Change the rules, if need be, to make the best of the team. Team first, always."

We were all set after the pep talk from Sulekha.

We all started the walk at her command. We walked to the best of our abilities as a team, hand in hand. But we also made sure that we were enjoying our walk as well. Win or lose, we didn't want to miss the beautiful moments – hand in hand, together, immersed in nature, as a team, enjoying and learning along the way.

We were almost done with Round 1, and then Round 2 would begin soon. Sulekha helped us with water and fruits as we enjoyed our walkathon. We were making good time, and soon we approached the last lap.

"Three cheers for everyone!" said Sulekha as we finished the last lap. Of course, she didn't know the timing of the other team. So, we didn't know whether we had won or lost, but as she mentioned, the celebration was not for the result, but the attitude with which we participated.

I felt it might have taken us almost an hour to finish all the ten rounds of this walkathon. I felt we did well. Sulekha noted the timings for each round.

"Good job, team," she said as she high-fived each one of us. The atmosphere was quite energetic, and it felt like we had just finished an Olympic race.

"I think we scored well. It's better than most of the earlier batches," commented Sulekha, while glancing through the round-wise scores that she had noted down.

All of us were glad and were very hopeful of winning. But at the same time, we were also aware that the batch with the Monk had better walkers, and then it was the Monk himself who was leading them. So, the competition was tough, and who knows what surprise was in store for us.

We slowly walked towards the lunch area, tired but confident, and a little tense about the result.

The Monk's team was not yet there, though that did not mean by any stretch of imagination that they hadn't yet finished the walk. They may be having fun after the walk, or just having a discussion, or perhaps they started late. The Monk must have noted the start and end time of the walk, and that was all that mattered.

After about ten minutes, the Monk's team also arrived, having a good laugh as expected. It would be interesting to know their timing. Curiosity was building up.

It was Sulekha who displayed our team's timing first.

"Okay, we took a total of fifty-one minutes and twenty-four seconds for ten rounds (51:24)."

We all cheered and clapped for our team. At the back of the mind, we knew it wasn't a particularly fabulous timing, but then, we waited for the Monk and his team to announce their timing.

"Okay, good job, Sulekha. Your team did well. We completed our ten rounds in a total of about fifty-five minutes and thirty-four seconds (55:34). You guys have won!" announced the Monk.

"Ohhhhhh noo..." moaned the Monk's team.

We had not only won, but had also won convincingly. We could not believe how it had happened.

And we clapped again and cheered. It was always remarkable to beat the Monk and his team. Everyone from the Monk's team came and congratulated us, shook hands and patted our backs.

We did have the fun part. But I was sure that there was something that we were still missing.

"But what is better – the victory or the defeat – is a matter of perspective," said the Monk.

He continued, "Defeat usually teaches us a lot more than victory. But that does not mean that we cannot learn from victories. Victories can teach us to re-emphasise our beliefs, and make our convictions stronger than ever before. So, Sulekha and team, please tell us what you think you guys did to win. We had better walkers, and probably had better strategies, but you won and won by a decent enough margin."

Sulekha complimented both the teams and said, "I think our conviction has been strengthened yet again today by the results of this race."

She continued, "The devil, as usual, is in the details. The answer is not obvious based on the overall timing but on the details of each round. Let me show you how we fared in each round of the race."

Something simple, and yet powerful, was coming up. This simple walkathon would end in an eye-opening lesson. Nothing happened at the Monk's place without a reason. He was ready to be defeated so that we could learn.

Sulekha showcased and started to talk about the round-wise timings that she had noted down during our walk.

Round 1: 4 min 54 sec
Round 2: 5 min 15 sec
Round 3: 5 min 25 sec
Round 4: 5 min 15 sec
Round 5: 5 min 02 sec
Round 10: 4 min 43 sec

And she halted after displaying all the numbers. She kept the register in front of all of us for us to have a look at the data and analyse it ourselves.

"So, what do you guys think?" asked the Monk after looking at the data. What is your analysis of why Sulekha's team won? Why do you think we failed in the walkathon?" the Monk asked his team while pointing to the data.

The Monk's team had not noted down the round-wise details, so it was difficult to compare the data between the two teams. So, the team was blank.

"I remember that Sulekha really charged us up in the last round," Kavita attempted to analyse the data.

"Yes, of course she must have. I can see from the last round data that you guys really pushed in the last round. But that could be just a 10-15 second improvement. In fact, we were also supercharged in the last round. The fact is, any team will give it their all in the last round. The question is, how does one round justify your winning the competition by such a comfortable margin of almost four minutes?"

We were clueless.

"Because we were tracking the round-wise data, and you weren't? Did that help us push harder subconsciously?" Kavita shot a guess.

"I think you have hit the bull's eye, Kavita," acknowledged the Monk.

"Are we saying that just tracking the data can help us do better?" Kavita tried to reaffirm what she had learnt.

"Yes, exactly, that's called the 'Miracle of Self-Monitoring'. Study the data once again very carefully, round by round, and tell me what you observe," said the Monk.

"We are improving with every round..." Kavita shot back while she was still glancing at the data.

"Right, and what if you slipped in one round?" asked the Monk.

"We recovered in the very next," Kavita was prompt to respond yet again.

"Excellent... why is this happening? I mean, you must be getting tired with each passing round, so why were you improving with every round? Was that your strategy to push yourself to improve with every round?"

"Not really, Sulekha just made us look at the timing after every round, but frankly, we did not make any specific efforts to get better. In fact, we had suggested to Sulekha that this would be an additional overhead and waste our time, and so we should drop the noting down of the timing, but she insisted. Now, we understand why," remarked Kavita.

"Yes," confirmed Sulekha.

"But how come this happens even if we don't make conscious efforts to improve?" I asked the Monk, interrupting the enlightening discussion between Kavita and him.

"Yes, that is an important question. You see, tracking is an external behaviour, but it unleashes some of our most powerful internal strengths, which are driven by the release of happy hormones inside our body," explained the Monk.

"Internal strengths? Like?"

"We will talk about them during dinner time, but for now, you must know that the miracle is in monitoring – whether it is race timing, weight reduction, preparing for a competitive exam, or controlling your expenses. If you are tracking it, you can be sure you are going to improve it."

"If tracking is the magic, then how come we underperformed in some rounds compared to the previous rounds?" asked Kavita, trying to analyse the data further.

"The improvements may not always be linear, but improvements will happen. That is true not only with what we track but in nature as well. How do you think that the temperature change happens with a season? Is it like consistent linear change, or are there some days which are against the trend? When you give mock tests while preparing for a competitive exam, do you think your score keeps improving with every practice test, or is it non-linear, and with an overall improvement? If you have faith in the Miracle of Self-Monitoring and are ready to push through non-linearity, you will see an overall improvement. You can apply the mantra of self monitoring to progress, to learn, to save more, to recognise patterns, find solutions, and overcome plateaus."

The Monk continued, "And this monitoring must be on paper or on a mobile application, but never in your mind. Your eyes must see it and take the entire pattern and trend inside you, for the inside hormones to be released and changes to be triggered."

"Really? So, are you saying that if we must improve our savings and reduce our expenses, we need to track and monitor them very closely?" I inquired.

"Yes, you are right."

But how long do we need to carry out such a level of intense tracking?"

"Forever. It must be a life habit, like brushing your teeth and bathing."

"Forever? But isn't this tough?" I could not visualise myself tracking my expenses month after month for the rest of my life.

"Yes, it is not easy for sure, but are you afraid of tough things?"

"No, but I am wondering whether we will have the level of discipline and focus needed for such a level of self-monitoring."

"It is not easy, but it is not complex as well. Yes, it demands discipline. It demands focus. It demands that you pay a price for it. Anything worthwhile in life demands a price. Is it easy being a Sachin Tendulkar? Or is it easy being a mother? Or is it easy being a Sergey Bubka? Nothing worthwhile is easy. In fact, it is unfair to ask the question whether a task is easy or not. A fairer question would be whether a task is worthy or not?" clarified the Monk.

We all listened in and tried to absorb the pearls of wisdom that kept pouring out of the Monk's sublime words.

The Monk continued, "So, is it worth pushing yourself into such discipline if that helps you experience freedom in life? Is it worth bringing that laser focus if it helps you pursue your dreams? You must answer this question. I cannot answer it on your behalf."

The Monk looked at his watch and, with a quick farewell, left for his hut.

He left us with this open-ended question around worthiness of any task, and the remaining lunch. We finished off our lunch at leisure. We were all excited and charged up. We all knew the answer to the Monk's question.

There was no activity planned before dinner, other than going to water a set of trees. So, we strolled back to our rooms to fill in the only learning card on the table.

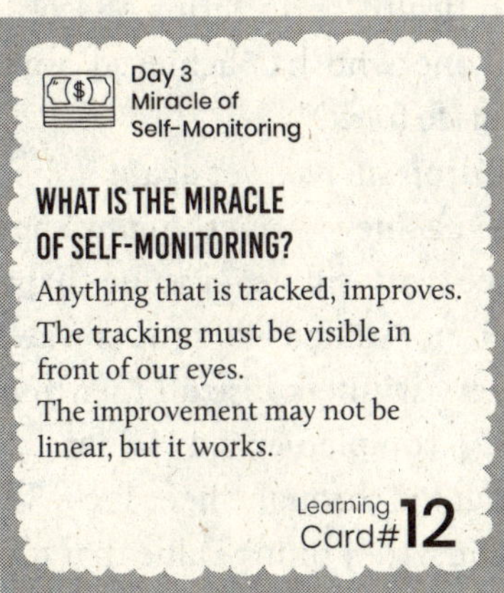

I kept pondering over this card for a long time. Was tracking really so important? Did it work every time? In every field of life?

Wasn't it boring to track? Weren't we going to waste too much time tracking our expenses? I had enough ammunition for dinner.

After a quick nap followed by the watering of the trees, we gathered in the lawn, chatting and discussing the Miracle of Self-Monitoring. Haider, amongst us, had good personal experience in monitoring and tracking his expenses and he shared how self-monitoring had helped him. But nothing like listening to the Monk. As the much-awaited dinner time approached, I jumped up with my thoughts.

"I thought a lot about the Miracle of Self-Monitoring and tried to visualise myself doing it, but it just doesn't seem to be the thing of our generation," I addressed the Monk.

"Sure, it's boring, and is neither sexy nor novel. But then, that is the price you pay for your freedom, for your dreams. Nothing worthwhile comes for free. Do you think your promotion comes free? Don't you pay the price for it?"

"Price for promotion? Really?"

"Yes, the price for your promotion may come in terms of ignoring your own health, or in terms of sacrificing your family time. Tell me, anyone who has achieved anything worthwhile without paying a price for it?"

There was pin-drop silence, yet again.

"And even if you achieve something by sheer luck, and don't have to pay its price, you will never value that thing in your life. And anything that is not valued will soon slip away from your life."

"Yes, most lottery winners lose all their money in just a few years post-winning," complemented Haider.

"Exactly. They got it through sheer luck. They didn't have to work hard for it. Thus, they didn't value that money. So, they lost it all." Monk continued, "Do you think that we, as a country, got freedom without paying a price for it?"

"Of course, not..." we responded in unison.

"Then how in the world do you think that your own personal financial freedom will come without paying a price for it?"

"I get it."

"And it's just not about boredom and not being cool or sexy. There are many other deeper reasons why people don't track their expenses."

"Really? Like?"

"Yes, our conscious minds pridefully tell us that we already know how much we spend every month. So, what's the point of writing it down and wasting our time doing this boring thing? And if our minds were accurate, there indeed wouldn't be much benefit in tracking," explained the Monk.

"So, our mind is inaccurate?" Varun asked.

"Yes, absolutely. In fact, the power of tracking to improve our lives arises precisely because our minds are riddled with limitations and excessively reliant on heuristics. We are distractible, forgetful, short-sighted, and easily influenced by external factors. As an example, many times people don't want to hear the truth because they don't want their illusions destroyed. This makes even the best-intentioned person more likely to go in circles than to make forward progress. Self-monitoring works because it activates your brilliant unconscious abilities instead of relying on your flawed conscious mind. Monitoring is tough love, the kind that tells us the truths we don't want to hear."

The Monk was at his sublime best. And we never wanted the discussion to end.

"Yes, you talked about the internal changes that happen inside our body when we start tracking our expenses. Can you please elaborate?" asked Chandra.

"It's not difficult to understand. As our eyes capture the trends and improvements, we not only become more aware, more focused, more reliable, more creative, and more motivated, but this also releases a hormone in our body – the happy hormone – called Dopamine."

I had heard this name 'dopamine' before, but that was all about it. I had no further clue about this hormone.

The Monk continued, "Of course, dopamine is released under many other situations like listening to music, meditation, going for a walk, having a laugh, cooking and the like, but seeing yourself improve consistently in any area is a big factor for the release of dopamine – be it in the area of reducing expenses and saving more, or in any other area like weight reduction, etc. When dopamine makes you feel good, you get even better at self-monitoring, and your mind instructs your body to try to do more of what you did to release dopamine. So, you want to track and monitor even further. This entire thing becomes cyclic, and soon, you see self-monitoring as an activity that rewards you with happiness. And being happy helps you not just with tracking, but it impacts every area of life positively. It becomes like an uncontrolled nuclear reaction or the magical compounding," explained the Monk.

Sometimes I wondered whether the Monk was God sent. I wondered how he seemed to know everything while sitting amidst an isolated jungle, while we had no clue about these nuances of life, though we were so connected with everything around us.

"It is interesting to know that tracking our expenses can help us feel happier in other areas of life as well. But I was just thinking from a larger perspective. I mean, aren't we getting too concerned about money? I mean, we've learnt from you that the purpose of life is to live it and enjoy it. But if we get bogged down by tracking our expenses, won't we become miserly and not enjoy life?" asked Chandra.

"That's an excellent question, Chandra," admitted the Monk.

"I also had the same doubt. I mean, won't our mindset always be that of a miser if we get so engrossed in monitoring and saving money?" Kavita supported Chandra's point of view.

"Great! Let me rephrase what you guys are asking. Is saving more money going to devoid us of the happiness that money can buy? Is that the right understanding of your question?"

"Yes!" Chandra and Kavita confirmed.

"So, there are two attributes to it. For some time, yes, you'd feel the need to make sacrifices until you get to freedom, and we talked about this in our pre-lunch session that freedom is not going to come free. It would involve breaking away from the herd, and that will be tough. Secondly, and more importantly, it's not about getting miserly, it's about getting frugal."

"Oh, are they different? I thought frugal is a mere fancy word for being a miser."

"Not at all, Kavita. They are completely different leagues. A miser would try and save money from everywhere – many times subduing his or his family's happiness even though it doesn't cost much. Actually, a miser is always hoarding money with no upper limit. He is in a race to accumulate and hoard as much as he can. A frugal person, on the other hand, would know where to put his money, what is important for his family, and what is not. A frugal person doesn't want to hoard unlimited money; he just wants enough. He knows the upper limit that is enough for him. He has a fixed goal post."

"That's interesting. Can you share some examples?" I asked.

"Sulekha is an exemplary example right in front of all of you."

We always knew that Sulekha was special. I was all ears.

The Monk continued, "She, at your age, was clear that she wanted to get a decent car, but not a luxurious car, even if she could afford it. She would rather save the ten lakh rupees. But when it came to her kids' education and upbringing, she was fine with spending an additional twenty lakhs. So, it's not that she didn't want to spend, but she was clear about where she wanted to spend. Typically, a frugal person gives more preference to family and long-term goals, rather than the herd-driven luxuries of life."

"Interesting... but that is for big events in life like buying a car or a house. Here we are talking about smaller monthly expenses. Won't we become miserly?" Chandra asked.

"Firstly, Chandra, do not underestimate the power of small. As we talked earlier, a ₹ 10 increase in savings is like a ₹ 50 increase in income. Secondly, the same idea of being wiser applies to the smallest expense of your life. You want to first become conscious of where you are spending more, and that can happen only when you consistently monitor. When you know where you are spending the most, then you get deeper to analyse if you can do something to avoid wastages in that area. It could be groceries, medicines, phone bills – anything. That's how you do it.

"Track → Analyse → Shortlist → Focus → Get deeper → Identify the wastage → Improve → Track

"That is how the cycle gets completed. So, in a nutshell, when we are getting frugal, we are getting smarter, wiser, efficient – the Kaizen way."

"Kaizen way? What is Kaizen?" asked Haider.

"You don't know Kaizen? We learnt it twenty years back," I jumped off with a response.

"Okay, but what is it?"

The Monk started to explain, "It is a Japanese term meaning to change for the better, or continuous improvement. It is a life philosophy that is also applied to businesses. The word 'Kaizen' itself comes from the Japanese word 'kai', which means change, and 'zen', which means good or virtue. The philosophy behind

Kaizen is that small, incremental changes routinely applied and sustained over a long period result in significant improvements."

"Ah, interesting!"

"And don't ask me how the Japanese became the world's number one economy after being devastated by World War II. They did not have the land, natural resources, people, skills, language, or anything. But they conquered the world, be it with their cars or electronics. They controlled the world for many decades."

"Kaizen alone cannot be responsible for this Japanese turnaround, right?", questioned Haider.

"Why not? Just because it is a small improvement?"

"Yes, I mean, Kaizen is good, but it cannot take them to the top of the world," argued Romesh.

"Of course, there were many other factors, but beware not to undermine the massive impact of the small. Once you understand the impact of the small, you will start appreciating that nothing is small. If you improve 1 per cent every day, how much better would you be after 365 days?" asked the Monk.

"Well, 365 per cent better, I think," responded Romesh.

"So, 3.65 times the earlier version, that is three-four times better?" the Monk asked Romesh.

"Yes"

"No, you would actually be 37 times, or 3700 per cent better."

"Really?" Romesh was shocked, as most of us were.

"Yes, that is compounding for you. Never ever underestimate the power of a small change when done consistently over time. And the same holds good for your expenses. Small expense improvements done consistently can bring your freedom closer by many years."

We were stunned and speechless.

"Okay, back to the happy hormone. And as you start releasing dopamine, this improvement cycle picks up pace. You start loving the process, and you start getting excited about the ensuing freedom."

We were left with empty plates by now, and still absorbing the deep knowledge being imparted here. We didn't even realise what we were eating, what was the taste or the aroma of the food being served. All our senses seemed to have converged into the wisdom that was being imparted by the Monk.

"C'mon, be frugal, Varun," the Monk said, pointing at Varun's plate with leftovers. "Not wasting food is being frugal, not a miser."

Varun obeyed and started gulping the leftover food hurriedly.

"Okay, we have an important announcement to make and it's urgent as well," remarked the Monk.

We listened in rapt attention.

"All of us have to go back to our huts, pack our backpacks and be ready to move."

"Move? Where?" I asked.

"We are all going to travel to Sulekha's house."

"Right now?"

"Yes, in the next half an hour. We have a bus waiting outside. It takes about an hour from here."

"But we are twelve of us. Will she and her family not be troubled?" Varun checked to make sure.

"She has a loving family. And we will sleep in the guest hall that she has for shameless people like us, who go over mostly uninvited," the Monk looked at Sulekha and we all had a good laugh. Sulekha seemed a bit tense though.

"Anything important happening there?" Varun checked further.

"Yes, one of her relatives is not well, and she needs to visit them urgently. She cannot wait until the end of this programme. And since it is impossible to run this programme without her active support, we thought we would just follow her."

"Oh, okay."

"This would also be a great opportunity for all of us to enhance our learning experience," remarked the Monk.

"Opportunity?" I asked.

"Yes, all the right awareness about saving money and getting rich cannot be imparted in the jungle. You all are city dwellers, and for some practical knowledge, we must confront ourselves and experience these principles in city life as well."

"That will be great." I was glad that we were truly having an enriching experience in the course of this programme.

"So, guys finish your packing, fill up your learning cards for the day, and report at the entry gate in thirty minutes. The bus will depart from there. Be on time please, since we do not want to cause too much trouble to her family."

"Sure..."

We returned, packed, and filled the learning cards.

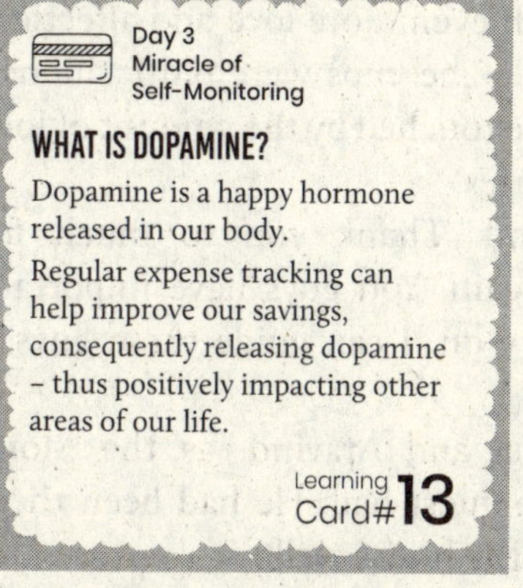

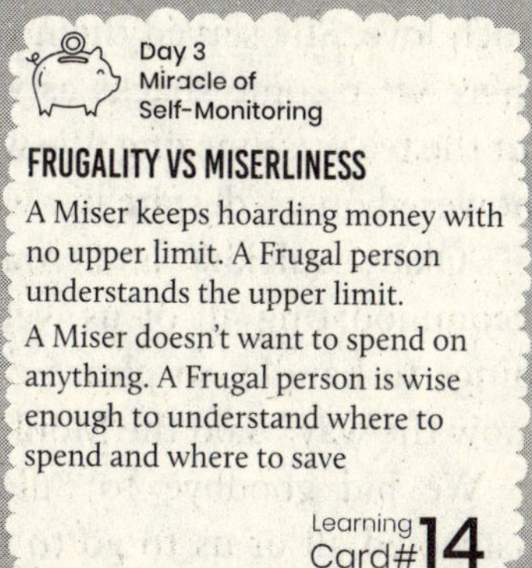

We all arrived at the gate in less than half an hour. The bus had arrived. It was a standard bus without any air conditioning, but comfortable enough. The bus reached Sulekha's home well on time. In fact, sooner than expected.

"Come on in..." Sulekha led the pack to her house. She welcomed and guided all of us to her drawing room.

It was a spacious room with hardly any furniture except for a brand-new sofa, which we were about to spoil. On the positive side, the hall had enough seating capacity for all of us. Other than this new sofa, all we could see were a few faded curtains neatly hung. The wall paint was decent, but of course, it did not match the newness of the sofa. The TV was small and was an older model. The centre table alongside the sofa was rugged and strong, but was kind of a misfit in the room.

"He is Aravind. He has been tolerating me for many decades now," Sulekha introduced us to her husband. We all stood up and greeted him.

"Raise your hands for tea, please..." Sulekha was back on duty the moment she entered the house.

Almost half of us raised our hands.

"And coffee?" The other half raised their hands.

Sulekha, assisted by Aravind, prepared the beverages with much love. She served them with even more love and affection. There were some snacks as well. The cups were old-fashioned but the tea was amazing. We were touched by the amount of love showered on us, despite her worries.

"Okay, Sulekha and Aravind. Thank you so much for accommodating all of us, yet again. You guys have important things to handle, so please carry on. I can guide these guys. I know the way," said the Monk.

We bid goodbye to Sulekha and Aravind, as the Monk instructed all of us to go to the guest hall. He had been there many times earlier and he knew the house well.

***

The guest hall was on the other side of the house – a big hall, big enough to accommodate all of us. The bedding in the room was placed as in a dormitory, but we didn't mind. We had become used to jungle life, and we were back in the city. So, anything was a luxury at the moment.

"Okay, guys, prepare for bedtime and go to sleep. We've got to wake up early in the morning and meet Sulekha before she leaves for her relative's place. And then we must go out for breakfast. Sulekha won't be available tomorrow morning. She will be leaving early in the morning. We must manage," the Monk had, so seamlessly, taken over Sulekha's role as our group coordinator.

"Okay, sounds good," we all said in a chorus. In no time, we were all fast asleep.

Day 4

AVOID THE TRAPS

I didn't sleep very well that night. Probably, we had got used to sleeping in the fresh air, with nature all around us. The Monk woke us up early and we freshened up in the common bathroom, and felt like college kids again.

We were soon back in the drawing room at Sulekha's house.

"The curtains don't match the bright sofa, no?" I couldn't keep my perfectionist spirit to myself and mentioned this to Varun.

"Yeah, you are right. Not that it matters to us, and with all due respect to Sulekha, but even the wall paint looks faded when compared to the brand-new sofa..."

The Monk was listening to our conversations as we waited for Sulekha

"Beware of the Diderot Trap, guys," remarked the Monk. His voice was loud enough for everyone sitting around us to hear.

I stared at Varun, and he stared back at me. "By any chance, are you talking to one of us?" we asked the Monk.

"Yes, to both of you."

"Actually, we didn't understand what you just said. Do you mind repeating it?" I asked the Monk.

"I said, beware of the Diderot Trap," Monk repeated slowly and in a clear voice.

"But what is this Diderot Trap? At least I have no clue," Varun confessed.

I looked around and found everyone as clueless as I was.

Meanwhile, Sulekha came in. "I had a long conversation with my uncle, and I must leave for the hospital right now. The good news is that my aunt is now out of the ICU, so I think I should be back by the evening to accompany all of you. We can return to our resort together."

We were glad.

"Sounds good, Sulekha. Please pass on our best wishes to your uncle. We all sincerely pray that your aunt gets well soon," the Monk patted and hugged Sulekha before she left.

"We will be going out to get some breakfast. We will bring it here and have it. And in the afternoon, we will go shopping so you can pick up some stuff for your families before you go back to the resort," the Monk addressed us.

"You were saying something about the Diderot Trap. Can we finish that discussion before we leave for breakfast?"

"Yes, sure, Harry. It just struck me when I overheard your discussions. This Diderot Trap is based on a true story, so let me share it with you," said the Monk.

When the Monk started to share, we all listened with open minds. These stories have been transformational for most of us so far.

"There was a famous French philosopher named Denis Diderot. He almost lived his entire life in poverty, but that all changed in 1765. At that time, Diderot was 52 years old, and his daughter was about to get married. But he could not afford to provide a dowry. Despite his lack of wealth, Diderot's name was well-known because he was the co-founder and writer of *Encyclopédie*, one of the most comprehensive encyclopaedias of the time. When Catherine the Great, the Empress of Russia, heard of Diderot's financial troubles, she offered to buy his library from him for £1000 GBP, which was a hefty amount for those times by any standard. Suddenly, Diderot became rich with this windfall and had a lot of money to spare."

"Much like we have money to spare when our salary goes up..." added Harry.

"Yeah, you are bang on, Harry, but shortly after this lucky sale, Diderot made the mistake of acquiring a brand-new scarlet robe. That's when everything went wrong."

"Everything went wrong because of one scarlet robe? Really?" asked a surprised Harry.

"Yes, Diderot's scarlet robe was beautiful. It was so beautiful, in fact, that he immediately noticed how out of place it seemed when surrounded by the rest of his common possessions. In his words, there was no more coordination, no more unity, no more beauty between his robe and the rest of his possessions. The philosopher soon felt the urge to buy new things to match the beauty of his robe. Money was, anyway, not a problem. So, he replaced his old rug with a new one."

"How interesting," I got actively pulled into the discussion.

"Now with a new robe and a new rug, he decorated his home with beautiful sculptures and a better kitchen table. He bought a new mirror to place above the mantle, and his straw chair was relegated to the antechamber by a leather chair," continued the Monk.

We listened in amazement, and most of us had an inkling as to where this story was headed.

"These reactive purchases, triggered by one new possession, have come to be known as the Diderot Effect. Essentially, obtaining a new possession often creates a spiral of consumption, which leads you to acquire more new things. As a result, we end up buying things that our previous selves never needed."

"Is this a true story?" asked Varun.

"Yes..." confirmed the Monk.

"But then, how does it impact us? I mean, I understand your point to be cautious with a new purchase, but I don't think we are that foolish that we will spend all our money on trying to match one new purchase," asked Harry.

"You have no idea how foolish humans can be. We are a highly overrated species. And it's not just about being foolish. In the pursuit of learning this art of saving money, we don't do things deliberately or out of choice. We don't even realise when we fall into the trap. We normalise such traps. Our mind gets things done unknowingly for us, just like it was perfectly normal to have matching curtains and the wall paint... remember?"

I was stunned and felt embarrassed when I realised what we had been discussing. The discussion was precisely about the Diderot Trap.

The Monk continued, "Sulekha got this new sofa since her earlier one was completely broken. Fine... money well spent. But the wall paint, the curtains, the television – they are working well. They need not be 'matched' with the freshness of the sofa. Be very careful when spending on one new thing, as it can have a spiralling effect unless you are very conscious about the Diderot Trap. Remember, even an enlightened philosopher fell for consumerism's allure. By understanding the Diderot Effect, we can make more intentional choices and avoid unnecessary upgrades that lead to financial strain and dissatisfaction. It can help us save more, invest more, and get to freedom faster."

"This is amazing. I can now relate this to my kids' school shopping this year," said Kulwant.

"Yes, it is applicable everywhere, Kulwant. Do you wish to share your experience of this trap for everyone's benefit?" the Monk asked Kulwant.

"Yes, sure. Actually, last week, my wife took my nine-year-old daughter shopping for the upcoming school session. On her shopping list was a new backpack. My daughter chose one. However, this new backpack obviously did not match the lunch bag she used last year, so almost immediately, a new lunch bag was added to the shopping list, even though her lunch bag was as good as new. I never realised that we were caught in the Diderot Trap then, but now I clearly do," explained Kulwant.

"See... and after the lunch bag, it would be a water bottle, and then a geometry box, and then shoes, followed by socks, and then a dress... It's tough to hold this spiral once it is triggered. Even before we realise that we are in a spiralling spending trap, we have done a lot of spending already. And the more you have spent, it becomes tougher to hold the further spiral," the Monk added on to what Kulwant explained.

Kulwant was looking worried, listening to the Monk's prediction of the spiral ahead.

"Hey Kulwant, that is okay... Try your best to hold it. We understand your stress." The Monk patted Kulwant, as we all had a good laugh.

"I can also relate to one such incident. Can I share it?" asked Romesh.

"Of course, that is what we are here for. Please go ahead Romesh," the Monk was glad that everyone was participating.

"I remember going shopping for a new t-shirt, and..." Romesh started to share his experience.

"And ended up with a new pair of jeans as well?" remarked Varun, even before Romesh could finish his sentence.

"Yes, you are right, Varun. The Diderot Trap yet again," confirmed Romesh.

"I also have something to share..." remarked Haider.

"Sure, go ahead..."

"When I think back and try to identify this trap, I can easily do so. I started working out last year. Now, for that, I had to buy a pair of shoes suitable for the gym. So far, so good, but none of my clothes matched what people wear at the gym, so I had to buy a top to match, and then some trousers. Then I proceeded to buy sweatbands and a new water bottle, Bluetooth headphones, and a yoga mat... and then... after all this was bought, I quit the gym."

We all laughed.

But behind this laugh was immense learning – a life-changing learning. Understanding the traps was the key. Awareness was the key. Staying away from the herd was the key. Self-monitoring was the key. Charting your own path was the key. Paying a price for your freedom was the key.

"Okay, guys, before you all cry with hunger, we need to fetch ourselves some breakfast from the nearby market. Follow me. I know the local market here... I will take you."

We all marched behind the Monk, with our latest learning being the discussion point. We were glad that we had time to share each other's experiences.

"Okay, it is about a ten-minute walk... hope it's okay with you all. Anyone who doesn't feel like walking can stay back and we will get the stuff for him or her. But remember that you are going to miss some learning on the way."

No one wanted to miss the learning, the time with the Monk, and of course, the breakfast.

"We are now used to much longer walks," I confirmed to the Monk on everyone's behalf.

"Yeah, I know... so let us get going. We will have to walk across the new road, and then onto the pavement till you see a temple in front. The market complex is just behind the temple."

We started to walk.

"You come here often?" I started chatting while walking alongside the Monk.

"I have been here a few times, primarily because Sulekha has been through a lot in her life."

"Oh really? She always looks so cool and easy going..." I was surprised to hear this.

"What you see and hear may not always be the reality. This is another important reason that we should break away from the herd, because the herd never reveals its true self, and we get influenced by what is shown to us."

"I get that. Is everything fine with her now?" I was genuinely concerned about Sulekha and her well-being.

"Well, she is coping. Her husband has been having an illicit affair with someone else. She will probably file for a divorce. She lost one of her daughters to a terminal disease, and has her own ailments to take care of. She has gone through a lot. But she is a fighter. She will only come out stronger."

We were all quietly walking along the way, led by the Monk. I couldn't believe what I had heard. Both Sulekha and Aravind never seemed like they were on the verge of separating. The Monk was right about the fact that what we see and hear may not always be the reality. We can all be so wrong in judging people and situations around us.

"This is the new road you said," remarked Kavita.

"Yes, Kavita, this road was carved out a couple of months back after massacring the flora and fauna around the earlier road."

I could sense the pain in the Monk's voice. And why not? We now understand it takes so much effort to plant and nurture every single tree. But in the name of growth and development, we cut down hundreds of them overnight and that too without any sense of guilt. In fact, we call that development. What a paradox of life.

"Really? Is this a new road? The traffic at this time in the morning makes us believe that this has existed for decades. I mean, how did this area survive a few months back? Where was this traffic diverted when this road was not there?"

"Nowhere..." replied the Monk.

"Nowhere means what? Are you saying that this is new traffic?" asked a surprised Kavita.

"Yes, exactly."

Sometimes, the Monk's replies made us feel foolish. But in most cases, there has been immense learnings as many of our long-held myths have got shattered.

We all paused before Harry finally asked.

"So, are we saying that people bought new vehicles because of this new road? Please don't say that this madness is true."

"This is true, and this is not madness. There is a complex relationship between demand, supply and consumption. And this phenomenon you are observing here is called Lewis-Mogridge Position."

"Lewis-Mogridge Position? What's that now?" asked Harry. And we all knew instantly that there was something new coming up. We were all ready to absorb.

"The Lewis-Mogridge Position is a microeconomic concept which tells us that as more roads are built, more traffic consequently fills these roads. Speed gains from the new roads can disappear within months, if not weeks," the Monk tried to explain in his simple words.

"Is there anything in the world that you don't know, Monk?" I just couldn't restrain myself.

"A lot... I am very clear that my awareness of these microeconomic concepts is limited to the idea of saving money. I have never studied economics, nor do I understand it fully," he admitted.

The Monk's honesty and simplicity had won our hearts many times over. This was just one more instance where we realised that there is so much to learn in this world, and there seemed to be so little time.

"Saving money? Now, what does the Lewis-Mogridge Position have to do with saving money?" Harry continued interrogating the Monk to satisfy his desire to learn from the horse's mouth.

"See, while this phenomenon was coined primarily for road infrastructure, in general terms, this is often referred to as 'Induced Demand'."

I thought I had heard about this earlier. Didn't the Monk talk about Induced Demand just a couple of days back? Or was that Induced Consumption? Were they the same? I was confused.

"Is Induced Demand similar to Induced Consumption that you talked about earlier?" I asked the Monk.

"This is an interesting question. They're related, but we must understand the relationship carefully. Induced Consumption, which we studied earlier, was because you had excess income and you were trying to chase the herd. You had money and enough of it. You had more money than you expected. And to comply with social pressure and herd mentality, you decide to spend that money. Induced Demand, on the other hand, typically gets triggered even without excess income or herd mentality. It's just more availability of the road network, of the products, of everything. When more of everything is available around you, you tend to latch on to it even if your savings come under pressure. Induced Demand can trigger Induced Consumption in the case of surplus money. They are both interrelated, and they both can trap you unaware."

"So, are we saying that we are consuming more because we have an increased supply of products and services?"

"What else do you think? Do you think we have started feeling so hungry that we want to get obese? Ask Haider."

We all laughed out as Haider placed his soft hands on his bulky tummy while enjoying the discussion.

We turned around the temple just following the Monk. The hustle bustle of the market was getting louder now.

"It's the supply which is creating the demand, and not the other way round. The product manufacturers understand that very clearly, and they make full use of it. Be watchful now before you reach the market. You will see so many products to consume, but stay focused on what is actually needed for breakfast. Don't fall for any 'Induced Demand'. Don't buy or eat just because it is available. Understanding the economic concept of Induced Demand helps you take your household expenses to reasonable and required levels. Lack of awareness of these economic concepts not only ruins your budget, but also harms your health."

We all understood and vowed to be careful.

"I will get some poha packed. You guys have any specific preference?" asked the Monk while standing near the cash counter of the restaurant.

"Let us have some dosas and idlis as well," Haider responded.

"Okay fine then, before I spoil you with choices and create any Induced Demand, let me place the order quickly. Four plates of poha, four masala dosas and five plates of idlis. All takeaway. We will wait here," Monk informed at the cash counter of the relatively small restaurant. He paid the entire amount and got the receipt before exiting the queue, allowing the next person in the queue to place his order.

We were waiting. A mix of all possible aromas had made us hungry. But the concept of Induced Demand was still fresh in our minds, and hence we were watchful. We didn't want to fall prey to Induced Demand anymore, especially if it was harmful for our health.

"Did you see what was kept near the cash counter?" asked the Monk.

We didn't really notice anything special, and thus the Monk answered his own question. "It's 'Induced Demand Trap'."

We all were very curious to see how an Induced Demand trap looks like. We all stared at the cash counter. The guy sitting at the counter looked very uncomfortable as so many pairs of eyes began staring at him. But most of us could not find anything of significance, except Haider.

"Are you talking about this box of chocolates?"

"Yes, Haider," replied the Monk.

He explained, "Most people who are ordering takeaway food at the counter are already hungry. They can just get the aroma while they wait. For those who cannot resist the temptation until the food is ready to be picked up, a chocolate can serve as a good filler. You also see that there is a box of paan as well, for those who are at the counter after eating are always tempted to have a paan after dinner. So, what is the restaurant guy doing here? He is inducing a demand for certain products. If you are not watchful, it is easy to fall prey to it."

"So dear, no biscuits, chips, cigarettes, paan or chocolates while we wait," Varun whispered in my ears.

"Not in front of him at least..." I whispered back to Varun.

But he heard it, yet again. How could we forget his super-powerful senses?

"No, don't constrain yourself because I am saying so... it's your life, it's your money, it's your goal. If you must save more to invest more and get rid of this maddening rat race and live a worthwhile life, only then should you pay this price; else, why pay this price at all? You are at will. My only job is to educate you. Who grabs what, implements what is their destiny and their choice. I do not control that, nor do I get influenced by it," the Monk clarified for everyone's benefit.

We felt a little embarrassed, and we knew that he was right. We quickly apologised for our behaviour.

"Why? Please don't apologise to me. Your behaviour doesn't make me sad or happy. It just impacts your life and the life of your loved ones. Chill out!" the Monk smiled and patted our backs.

He was a strange guy. Good or bad, it did not have an impact on him. He always wore a smile on his face. Was he truly human? Didn't he have feelings? No doubt, 'monk' was the right term for him.

The rest of the group was having a different discussion altogether. One had picked up a cigarette. Another a packet of chips.

"See, I was conscious of Induced Demand, and I decided not to have that packet of fried chips and take care of my health. I picked up this packet of healthy baked chips rather than the regular ones. This one also has fewer preservatives and more protein," justified Romesh as he showed the nutritional content section at the back of the packet to the Monk.

"Congratulations!" responded the Monk without even caring to look at the nutrients.

I wasn't sure whether he was being sarcastic.

"No really, this is healthy. I picked three packets of it, one for now, and two for later consumption as well. I want to be like you when I grow your age. I want to be fitter and healthier. So, no more junk," Romesh insisted.

"Yes, this is the expected behaviour of an alert consumer. You just displayed the Snackwell Effect," replied the Monk.

The crunching noise of the chips became conspicuous in the sudden silence of our group. Romesh slowed down his eating. He realised that he had probably made a blunder, though he didn't know what exactly was wrong with picking up a packet of healthy chips.

"What is the Snackwell Effect now?" I asked at the risk of more bashing for Romesh.

"Sir, your order is ready..." announced the restaurant owner, even before the Monk could respond to my question.

Monk and I picked up the bulk order, and we started on our walk back to Sulekha's home.

Romesh felt a sigh of relief and started to munch on his healthy chips again. While Romesh was still munching his way back, the Monk started explaining the Snackwell Effect.

"When faced with the so-called healthier food options, individuals tend to consume more of these items than they would of regular food options. This behaviour is driven by the belief that healthier foods won't harm us, or harm us far less. Essentially, it's like granting oneself a free pass to indulge more."

"But, this is healthy. You have a look at the ingredients," Romesh protested.

"It is not healthy," the Monk replied without looking at the ingredients.

"It is... You see this..."

"It is not healthy. It is just healthier than the junk you used to have earlier. But it is not healthy."

"Yeah, so it is healthier," said Romesh.

"Yes, in other words, it is less junk compared to the junk you used to eat earlier. But here is the challenge. It is, say, 20 per cent less junk, agreed. But now that you already had one pack and took along two packs since it is less junk, you are consuming three times the 'healthier' food than what you would have normally consumed of the other pack," the Monk continued, and we knew that Romesh would lose this argument.

"So, if you used to have 100g of junk food earlier with the fried pack, now you have 80g of the baked packet, but you have three packs instead of one. Essentially, now you are consuming 240g instead of the 100g earlier – a typical Snackwell Effect. Not only do you consume more, but you also spend much more. The 'healthier' food costs you more than the fried one. And make it three times the price because you consume more. As you consume more, you feel good that you are eating healthy, but you spend more and save less."

"So, are we saying that we consume more because we believe that it won't harm us?"

"Absolutely, we consume many times more for the incrementally healthier option. Healthier here means less junk. It is not healthy."

"That's an insight. I agree that we need to be more careful while snacking next time," I tried to end the discussion and accept defeat. It always felt good to learn new stuff from the Monk. Such a defeat was always welcome."

"It's not just about snacking, my friend. The Snackwell Effect hits you in every sphere of life. Again, don't go by the word 'snack'. It originated from the concept of snacks, but then, you have to be watchful of the Snackwell Effect in many other areas of life so that you can not only save your health, but also save a lot of wealth." The Monk was in no mood to stop.

"An example? Where else do you see the Snackwell Effect?" Varun inquired.

"You guys think about it... in your homes... do you have any energy-efficient devices?" triggered the Monk.

"Yes, we bought an energy-efficient AC last year," responded Varun after a bit of thinking.

"So, remember that it uses less energy than the previous AC model, right. But that is beneficial if you use this AC for the same number of hours as earlier. But if this energy efficiency pushes your mind to the Snackwell Effect, you are likely to become careless about the number of hours you use your AC for the same reason, and ultimately, it might inflate your electricity bill," explained the Monk.

"Well, our bill hasn't gone up, but neither has it come down. So, we were wondering whether these ACs are truly efficient, or it is just a marketing gimmick," mentioned Varun.

"No, the ACs are effective. That is tested and verified, but probably that efficiency is compensated by more usage."

"Hmm... that is a really interesting perspective."

"The same goes for other efficient appliances at your home – the TV, electric bulbs, washing machines, etc.," explained the Monk.

"Wow... interesting."

"Look at that car..." the Monk pointed out the car at the traffic signal. It was a new red coloured sedan.

"The traffic signal is red and will remain so for the next 90 seconds as per the traffic signal timer. Right?"

"Yes..." we acknowledged.

"Yeah, but you see the driver is not concerned with switching off the ignition. He knows that this is a fuel-efficient car, which it is. It uses less fuel, so it might just be fine to let the engine run idle until the traffic signal turns green. If he were using an old, poorly efficient car, he might have switched it off. Not only is he wasting fuel in a fuel-efficient car, but he is also probably causing more harm to the environment as well."

"Interesting. So, a fuel-efficient car may actually be more harmful for the environment," I acknowledged.

"It can be, if we are not watchful of the Snackwell Effect. It plays out in almost every sphere of life. You just need to observe the world around you more attentively."

We looked at each other and just admired the Monk's way of observing the world around him.

The entire way back to Sulekha's house, we kept observing cars and traffic signals, and realised how prevalent the Snackwell Effect was. As soon as we reached Sulekha's home, we wasted no time and pounced on our breakfast.

"Each one on his own!" shouted the Monk, and let everyone get their share. Of course, as usual, the Monk skipped breakfast.

"Okay guys, listen on, for the post breakfast schedule which Sulekha has left us," the Monk started reading a note while we were still relishing the meal.

"So, after we are done with breakfast, we have around three hours to visit the Keruchu local market. It's a market twenty minutes away from here. We can buy local groceries for Sulekha's family. Make sure you keep the Induced Demand and Snackwell Effect in mind while you shop."

"Yes... Okay... sounds like a good plan," I confirmed on behalf of everyone.

"And Sulekha was also kind enough to arrange the next set of learning cards for you guys. She is just amazing. Even during adversity, she is thinking about all of us," announced the Monk, as he pointed towards the cards.

We had absolutely no doubt about Sulekha's commitment to her work.

But this was perhaps for the first time that the smile was less prominent on the Monk's face. He didn't seem his radiant best. Were Sulekha's family issues bothering him as well? Or was there something else? Or maybe I was overthinking, over-analysing and trying to read too deep.

It was just fair to let it go, at least for the time being.

We took our own spaces in the drawing room – some of us on the sofa, some on the floor. We made the best use of our time in recapping our learnings of the day so far.

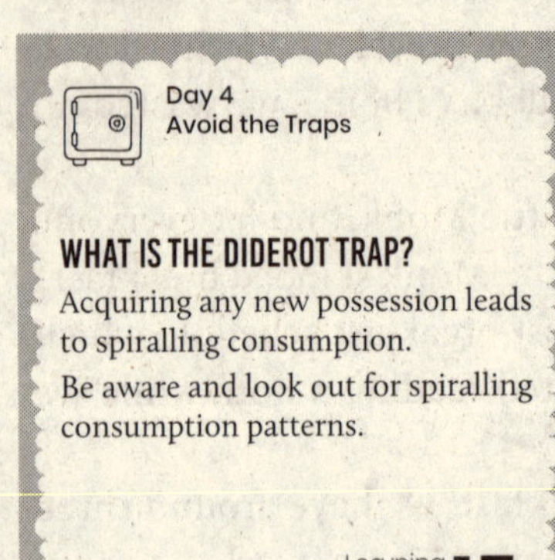

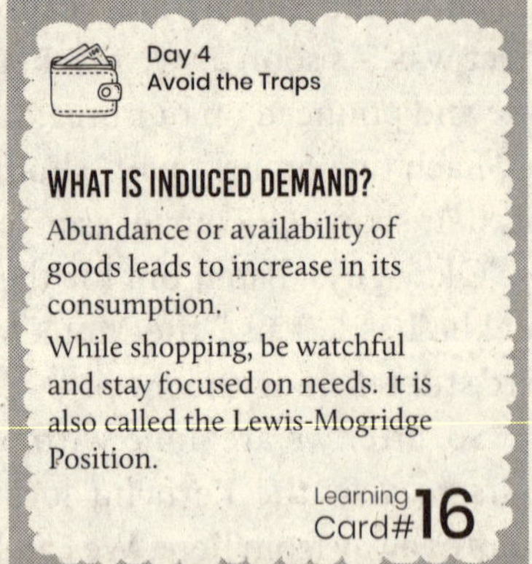

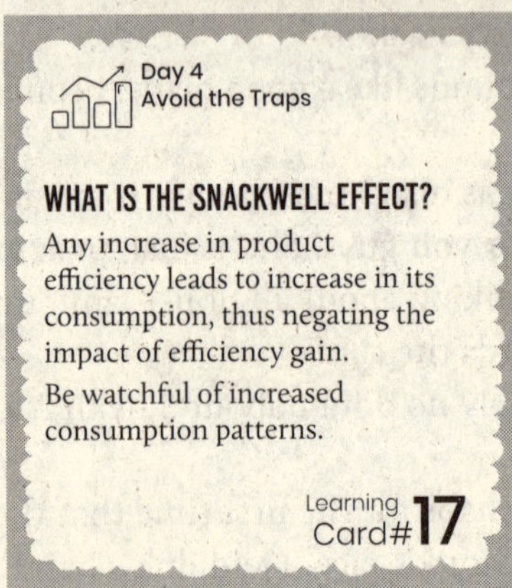

We felt very satisfied looking at all our previous learning cards. It was such an excellent way to recap what we had learnt. I thought it just made imbibing the learning so much easier. The seventeen learning cards were akin to valuable treasure for me.

By now, some of us had started to feel sleepy, but then we picked ourselves up. We had to. There wasn't much time.

"Guys, let's move before it gets too hot," warned the Monk.

"Yes, let's go," we agreed.

"But have you done the Tri-Check?" he asked us.

"Now, what's that, Monk? Haven't ever heard of a Tri-Check earlier in my life," I commented.

"Good, your life is successful if you are learning new stuff every day. Do you know that any rocket launch goes through some of the most stringent checks in any industry?"

"Okay... that is quite understandable. But are we launching a rocket right now or going grocery shopping?" I pushed back. Sometimes, the Monk would throw a tangential statement at us, which would subsequently converge to make sense.

"I mean, it's years and years of hard work, billions of dollars, many careers, and sometimes lives at stake before a rocket is launched. And just one minor error is all it takes to bring all those efforts and money crashing to zero. Of course, scientists learn something new from every crash, but the mistakes are just too costly."

"Okay, that's interesting news, but shall we go shopping? We can probably discuss this on the way?" Varun reiterated. Like most of us, he didn't want to be late and then be forced to go out in the heat.

But the Monk was not ready to give up on his tangential topic.

"Rockets also undergo a Tri-Check. We cannot afford to go shopping without the Tri-Check."

"We are going grocery shopping, Monk. C'mon, that's nowhere close to a rocket launch, at least as per my current understanding."

"I know, saving money is not a science, let alone rocket science, but it is an art. And art demands that you go deep into understanding the human mind and its psychology. That is why it is important to do the Tri-Check before we leave for grocery shopping."

We were silent. Something interesting was about to be shared, as always.

"A Tri-Check, as the name suggests, is a three-step checklist. Whenever you go shopping, you must follow this simple process of doing an inventory check, preparing a shopping list considering the available inventory, and then sticking to the list when you go out shopping."

"Hmmm... does it really help?" We all thought that this was too simple a thing to compare it to a rocket launch. But we have also learnt that simple is powerful.

"Again, do not underestimate the power of small savings. We talked about it earlier. But it makes the entire process more efficient. It saves you money. But above that, it saves you time while shopping. It helps you avoid missing out on some essentials which you may need on another trip. It prevents you from buying what's already there at home. It just makes your fridge and your house a lot cleaner and more organised. It enhances your mood. It creates dopamine. It makes your day. It just triggers a chain reaction. You can never accurately map the significant tangible and intangible benefits you derive from such small efficiencies that you bring into your day-to-day life."

"Wow.... is this Tri-Check only applicable to grocery shopping?" Varun asked.

"No, you can apply the Tri-Check to any regular repeated shopping – grocery, clothes, stationery, gifts, vanity items, among others. All discretionary purchases fall under this, and some non-discretionary as well."

"Cool... excited to know the first of the tri-checks."

"Sure, as the first step, go ahead and check the inventory in the kitchen and the fridge. Then come back here and prepare the list. You can divide yourself into two teams – one doing the inventory check and the other preparing the list," directed the Monk like an army general directing his troops.

We obeyed. The kitchen team opened drawers and we were sitting on the new sofa with a pen and paper shouting the names of items likely to be required by Sulekha and her family. She needed help and we were happy to do our bit. The items which were already in the inventory - kitchen or fridge - were not written on the list and the rest were noted down.

We all worked like a well-oiled army unit, and in just a few minutes, the list was ready. Stages 1 and 2 of the Tri-Check were successfully completed. We presented the list to our commander.

"Great team, let us go shopping now. I repeat. Never ever go out without this list in your hand. Stage 3 is the most difficult by the way. Let's see if we can stick to the list. Stage 3 is where we apply the theory of Stages 1 and 2 in actual practice," directed the Monk.

***

We stuffed ourselves into the bus that drove us to the local shopping area. Once we deboarded, we began to indulge ourselves in no time.

"Okay guys, we will try and stay as a team as far as possible. We might learn a few things while we shop. Who has the checklist?" asked the Monk.

"Me!" shouted Haider.

"Okay, Haider, you will always stay with us. Do not wander around. You are the authority. Anyone with the checklist is the authority. You must authorise every single purchase. No one can purchase anything unless they are authorised to do so. Is that clear to everyone?"

"Yes, sir!" Most of us saluted the Monk.

And we went about the checklist-based shopping as prescribed by the Monk. There were times when we did slightly deviate from the checklist, but we were able to generally stick to it. For any deviation, of course, we took the approval from Haider.

After the mega success of the Tri-Check list, we had quite a few grocery bags in our hands. Sulekha would be so proud of us if she knew that we applied Tri-Check for her groceries.

We were back in the bus and started towards Sulekha's home. The Monk began meditating on the bus.

How can one meditate in a moving bus? I thought to myself.

But then, probably that was why he was a monk. The Monk meditating didn't surprise me as much as the tears flowing from his eyes while meditating did. I just nudged Varun while staring at the Monk and diverted his attention to the Monk's face. Varun also looked surprised by the tears, but we didn't want to disturb the Monk. I was not sure why he was so sad. He was a Monk. He had already lost his family. He seemed so happy while we were among the huts and in the jungle. I have seen him disturbed once earlier in Sulekha's house the previous day, and now I was watching him cry. I was not sure what was going on. Was he sad? Was he missing his family? Was there any other problem? Was everything fine with Sulekha's relatives, or was this just the next level of meditation? Who knows. But then, I didn't have the guts to ask him, at least at that moment.

Soon we were back at Sulekha's home. Kavita and Kulwant were good cooks, and they took over the kitchen to make lunch. While we were chatting in the drawing room, the Monk arrived from the washroom. There were no more tears, and he seemed to be back to his active best.

Chandra started the discussion, keeping himself focused on the programme agenda.

"So, this Tri-Check was very nice, but that is only applicable for frequent regular purchases only, right? I mean that is my understanding since we need to do an inventory check, make a list and stick to the list. But what about big purchases or non-frequent purchases, or rather, I should say, non-discretionary purchases? Is there something as useful as the Tri-Check for such big discretionary purchases?"

"Yes, we do have a Frugal Toolkit for all such discretionary, bigger and irregular purchases. We call it Quadra Kit," responded the Monk.

"Quadra Kit? Interesting, please tell us more," requested Haider.

"A Quadra Kit is essentially a set of tools or rules that help you stay frugal. If you remember, we understood that being frugal is not being a miser. It's just about avoiding wastage and being smart."

"Yes."

"Right, so being smart also means being aware of the tools at your disposal and making use of them."

"Great... and when would you explain this to us, Monk?" Haider was unable to hold his excitement.

"Excuse me..." the Monk got a call and he had to break away from the group. He was back in less than a minute.

"Okay team, the update is that I just got a call from Sulekha, and she'll also be joining us for lunch. And after lunch, we can return to the resort. On the way back, we will stop at a small complex where you can buy some gifts for yourself and your family. We can apply the Quadra toolkit while we shop at the complex, since buying gifts are a typically discretionary expense."

"Great. Learning it through a practical lesson is truly wonderful," said Haider, and we all agreed.

Kavita and Kulwant not only prepared lunch but also made sure that it was served with utmost grace. They were skilled and passionate about cooking. The aroma of the lunch was pulling us, but we were just waiting for the Monk to formally announce it open before we could pounce on it. And the Monk didn't make us wait too long.

"Three cheers for Kavita and Kulwant. This truly smells good and looks delicious. I don't think any of us can wait long enough. But thank you from the bottom of our hearts. You guys are incredible," the Monk raised a toast for both of them.

"Thank you, Monk. Anytime!" acknowledged Kulwant.

"Thank you, Monk. Your words mean a lot to us," added Kavita.

"Shall we go ahead then?" the Monk invited Kavita and Kulwant to get going first and do the honours.

And we did not have to wait any longer. While engrossed in our food, we saw the Monk's face light up as he looked towards the door.

And there she was. Sulekha was the only one who could bring cheer to the Monk.

"And three cheers that Sulekha is back among us," the Monk said, smiling.

"Three cheers!" we all shouted and welcomed her.

Before she started her lunch, Sulekha thought it was important to give us an update.

"So, my aunt is now out of the ICU. She should be able to recover and go back home in a week's time. So, I am relaxed and ready to return."

She continued, "And thank you for what you did in my absence. Grocery shopping, this lunch, and the aroma are just incredible. It's going to be difficult to stop indulging myself," Sulekha pointed at the lunch.

"You must thank Kavita and Kulwant for all this. We just got the groceries, but they converted the raw into something that was truly tempting," the Monk made sure that credit went where it was truly due.

"Of course! Both of you should stay here forever. I need a lot of help every day. I am not that good at cooking."

We had our share of laughter.

And then, Sulekha turned her face towards the Monk. Her smile vanished. She tried to smile but she looked sad and gloomy. And slowly, the Monk's face also turned sad. There was definitely something that both Sulekha and Monk knew that we had no clue about. Not that it was our prerogative to interfere in their personal lives, but most of us were genuinely getting concerned. It was so clearly visible on their faces.

"This lampshade is very beautiful. It gives an antique look to your drawing room," I told Sulekha trying to divert her attention from the pursuing tension with the Monk.

"We are glad that we didn't replace it with the new one," responded Sulekha.

"Why would you replace it with anything new? The new ones are not as pretty, seriously," I supported her decision.

"Yeah, we also feel that now. We didn't have access to the Quadra Kit tools at that point. So, it was quite natural to make that mistake. But I would say that we learnt about the tools in time from the Monk, and now, we fully appreciate that it was an awesome decision."

"Oh! So, was that decision a part of the Quadra Kit?"

"Yes, sorry, Monk, I am disclosing the first tool of the Quadra Kit right now..." Sulekha said in an apologetic tone.

"No, that is perfectly fine. Go ahead, please, Sulekha."

"So, guys... I learnt that the first tool in the Quadra Kit is to 'Delay your purchase'. This is especially true for a discretionary purchase like this lamp shade replacement."

"Delay the purchase? Is it? Does it really help?"

"Yes, as you can see in this case, we just delayed the lamp replacement by a couple of weeks since it was not urgent anyway. Similarly, if you feel the urge to purchase something discretionary, it makes a lot of sense to wait it out for at least a couple of weeks. Chances are that the desire to possess that item will pass, and if not, this would be an excellent time to think about whether it is worth spending money on! In many cases, in these two weeks' time, you might see some other expense which is more important in your life, and then this discretionary expense will go down your priority list."

"Hmmm... that is interesting... just delay the purchase," pondered Romesh.

"Right, what also happened in our case was that we started seeing the good things in the existing lamp. We cleaned it up, made it more presentable, put a decent matching cloth below it, and it suddenly looked pretty nice – and as you say, looked antique. By this time, the decision was taken to never replace it."

"That's a great story behind this antique lamp."

"Yeah, this was the first tool of the Quadra Kit that the Monk taught us – Delay, delay, delay, delay, delay, the big purchases which are discretionary. The bigger the purchase, the more it should be delayed."

"So, what if this lamp had stopped working? Would you replace it in that case as well?"

"You may have to make your assessment. If the cost of repair justifies its life after repair, then we would have gone ahead and repaired it. But if we felt otherwise, then we might have to replace it. But then, waiting is a must. A lot of new ideas pop up while waiting."

"Cool, the first tool of Quadra Kit sounds interesting – Delay the Purchase. And watch out for things to unfold," agreed Varun.

"Yes, emotions are volatile, just like the investment markets. If we have patience, we need to control our purchase impulses at the peak of our emotions, and we will see sanity even without the purchase. It might not happen in all cases, but our experience is that it happens in as many as half of the cases with us," said Sulekha. She sounded as apt as the Monk when dealing with personal finance and the art of dealing with money.

"Interesting... but I have an experience to share," said Harry.

"Sure, go on, Harry. Practical experience sharing is always very insightful."

"Sure. But my experience is not directly related to the purchase of goods, but the importance of having a delay in our emotions."

"Oh, that will be even more interesting. We are all ears," said the Monk.

"My wife and I used to struggle a lot a few years back because of consistent arguments, debates, and even verbal abuses when the arguments got very heated. As you understand, this often results in a stressful atmosphere at home. Our daughter was the biggest victim in this scenario." Harry was kind and courageous enough to share something so personal to him.

"Yeah, go on," I said.

"Right. So, both my wife and I wanted a solution, but we just couldn't control our outbursts. Then we happened to attend a seminar by Stephen Covey, a renowned author. Apart from all the other good things that we learnt in that seminar, there was one line that got stuck in both our minds, and eventually became our life changer," continued Harry.

"Yes, that is all you need. One word, one line, one sentence, one feeling, one emotion – that can change the course of your life. That is all we should be looking for from any session, seminar, book, movie, or a programme like the one we are currently in. That is enough return on your time and money investment. Do not try to learn too much. One powerful takeaway, which can be implemented in life, is a great takeaway," added the Monk.

"Sorry for this interruption, Harry, but it was important at this point. Please go ahead and share what you learnt and how it changed your family's future," said the Monk in an apologetic tone to Harry.

"Yes, I understand. Our biggest learning was that after every trigger that comes to us, there is always a minuscule time gap where we prepare our response to the trigger. In most cases, and as it was in our case, that time gap is too small for any logical or rational thinking. Our responses to such triggers are often instantaneous, coming out of our emotions, which we hardly have any control over, at least at that moment. Stephen suggested that if we could somehow increase this time gap between the trigger and the response, things would automatically change drastically for the better. His suggestion was very simple. Do not do anything complex. Just try to delay the response. That's it. If today, you respond instantly, try to respond after a ten-second gap, then slowly try to increase this delay to a twenty-second gap. Take it as a challenge for yourself. Try to delay the response and keep increasing the delay to minutes, then hours, then days. Forget about delaying the response for days, Stephen mentioned that if you can delay your response and take it to hours, then you may not actually need any response. The one who sent the trigger will likely apologise for their behaviour under the burden of guilt."

"Oh, wonderful... and what was the outcome? Were you able to delay the response?" asked Sulekha.

"Yes, with practice, we were able to get better at delaying our responses. And this one simple act of creating a delay in the response has brought about a sea change in our relationship. The interesting aspect is that there is no dearth of triggers even today. Life squeezes us, puts us under pressure, and triggers come from one of us. But what has changed is the fact that even if one of us throws a trigger, the other person goes on mute for some time, trying to delay the response. And often, in that mute phase, the person who created the trigger itself feels that the trigger was unwarranted and unnecessary. Often, the one who initiated the trigger itself apologises, and then there is no need for a response at all. This delaying technique has made our relationship much smoother and stronger," concluded Harry.

We all clapped at this story. It was heartfelt and touched each one of us.

"Awesome. The delay in response eases our emotions, and it is so beautifully narrated by Harry. And the same thing happens with the emotion to buy new stuff. If we can just delay the response, the trigger itself is likely to die out," Sulekha said.

We all looked at Harry and gave him a thumbs up.

"I have tried this delaying technique once on our purchases, but failed miserably. We just could not hold on for a few weeks, and we gave in to the purchase," remarked Chandra, sharing his personal experience.

"I am sure Harry didn't succeed the first time, or even during the second or third. It is a continuous process of self-improvement. The same with new big purchases. It is not easy to break the herd. It is not easy not to spend while you have the money. To push yourself through this waiting period, take it up as a challenge. I have done several of these challenges in the past, and they are so much fun! The rules involve spending no money for a specified period. If you can hold yourself accountable for this challenge, it will be an eye-opening experience that forces you to realise how often we buy things that are never needed in the first place. The satisfaction that comes from realising that we never wanted a particular thing, and we were able to control our emotions and make that work is unmatched," explained Sulekha.

"Hmmm..."

"Okay, guys, I won't steal any more thunder from the Monk's toolkit. I think we should do justice to the awesome lunch by Kulwant and Kavita. Attack, guys!"

As if we needed any further invitation from anyone, we were already feeling so hungry. Sulekha was having lunch with the Monk, and I noticed that they didn't speak a word to each other the entire time!

Maybe, I was overthinking or over-analysing. But then we got so engrossed in the delicacies on the table, I dismissed my thoughts.

"Wow, hats off to both of you, Kavita and Kulwant!" stated the Monk.

"Truly..." we all agreed.

By the time lunchtime was over, we all had over eaten and consequently, we started to feel sleepy.

But then the Monk wouldn't let us get lethargic.

"In ten minutes, we must leave for the resort. The bus is ready. And of course, Sulekha is also joining us."

"I am glad as I love each one of you," added Sulekha.

"We are too!" responded Monk on behalf of all of us.

"Now that I am back in action mode, let me give you some homework for these ten minutes. The purpose is to make sure that you do not feel sleepy," mentioned Sulekha.

We all smiled and were glad about her involvement in the art of learning to save money.

"Learning cards?" I shouted.

"Bang on, Manish. You are right. There is just one learning card, but that should be good enough to keep you awake. Pick up your card from the table and fill it up before we leave."

And we went turn by turn, picked up our new learning card, and started to fill it up.

I added this card in the repository and this bunch of cards felt like a gold mine in my hands – my takeaway from this wonderful programme.

***

We all boarded the bus, and the bus started off as per schedule. We halted midway at a small shopping centre. As we stepped out of the bus and started glancing at the shops and the stuff they stocked, we realised that this was kind of a 'chor bazaar' or a thief market in literal terms.

This place had some expensive-looking stuff available at very reasonable prices. As we walked down the market, we realised that these were probably imported, rather than smuggled into India.

Varun and I walked down the market together, looking at what the shops had to offer.

"This is the Buddha statue I always wanted for the entrance of our house. I saw it in my boss's house as well. It looks awesome with the lighting," I mentioned to Varun, stopping at a shop.

"Yeah, looks good. It's classy and gives a very antique look," remarked Varun.

"What's the price?" I asked the shop owner.

"₹ 10,000, sir."

"Isn't it too costly?" I asked Varun.

I was actually shocked at hearing the price. But then, I had no experience of buying anything similar earlier. I had only seen such a statue in houses where the owners were well off. So, maybe, it was worth the price.

"Not sure bro... I have no idea," came the expected response from Varun.

The Monk and Sulekha happened to pass by and couldn't help but overhear us.

"Okay, this is the perfect time to talk about the second tool of our Quadra Kit," intervened the Monk.

We turned around and saw the Monk smiling.

"And what was the first tool in our Quadra Kit?" asked the Monk.

"Delay the purchase," I shot back. "But I do not want to delay this purchase because I need to get something for my home, and I have always wanted this," I responded, trying to convey that I had already applied the first tool of the Quadra Kit.

"I understand," said the Monk as he led us away from the shop where we saw the Buddha statue. It seemed that this was going to be a slightly longish discussion.

He continued, "If you are sure you should not delay this purchase, and you have been trying to buy such a product for a long time, use the second tool from the Quadra Kit which suggests us that we need to make sure that we estimate the 'Intrinsic Value' of the product we wish to buy. Right now, you are being influenced by the 'Sign Value' of the product."

"Okay, hold on... got to understand this. What is 'Sign Value' and what is 'Intrinsic Value'?" I wanted to be very clear.

"Yes, of course, Manish. Let me share an example to help you better understand. Imagine a person purchasing a Rolls-Royce limousine. While the primary purpose of the car is transportation, its value extends beyond mere functionality. The buyer may also appreciate it as a symbol of wealth, a sign that communicates their affluence to a specific community and society at large. In this scenario, the car's transport function represents its Intrinsic Value, while its social prestige function gives rise to its Sign Value."

"Okay, so are we saying that Sign Value is mainly a symbolic value?"

"Yes, it makes sense for those who want to buy it as a symbol. It has nothing to do with the usefulness of the car."

"Okay, I can understand what you say when you talk about an ultra-luxury product like a limousine, but why do you think that I am influenced by the Sign Value of this simple Buddha statue?"

"You are influenced because you have seen it at your boss's house, you have seen it in the houses of other friends who are relatively richer. Your mind has associated this Buddha statue with a sign of wealth. It is like seeing the statue, and your mind tells you that it is about the rich and successful. This internal mind mapping is already done, and this pre-existing mind map is making you biased and deviated from the actual Intrinsic Value of the product."

"Interesting, but don't you think that products are usually priced as per their worth, more or less. I mean, you do expect that a Mercedes-Benz is costlier than a Maruti Wagon R, no?"

"Yes, a brand has a show-off value. And of course, you will get enhanced features and superior quality, but how much value is the point? We know that a Benz has better features and quality than a basic Maruti car, but how much better is the question."

"Isn't that value driven by a demand-supply curve?" I tried to catch the Monk on his strength – the economics of saving money.

By this time, most of the participants had gathered around the Monk and Sulekha, each one of us trying to absorb the nuances of the art of saving money. This was deep. Everything was happening inside our mind. It was not easy.

"That is an interesting point. Some goods are driven by a standard demand-supply curve, but not all," responded the Monk, and this came as a surprise to me and many other participants. With our limited knowledge of economics, we all thought that the market prices were always driven by a demand-supply curve.

"How does that work? I mean if there is no demand, the price will come down, no?" I immediately objected.

"I think this is just the right time to talk about the 'Tri-goods'."

"Tri-goods?"

"Yes, Tri-goods. There are three types of goods, especially branded goods, and you should be aware of them when you go shopping for expensive brands. This may not be relevant to this statue, but you will find it useful in setting the right perspective, rather than blindly following the brand."

"Okay." And we waited to hear about yet another economic theory that could potentially help us save big money.

"The first of the Tri-goods is the Ordinary Good, which qualifies as per your set pattern of demand and supply. Ordinary goods are goods that experience an increase in quantity demanded when the price falls, or conversely, a decrease in quantity demanded when the price rises. This is in line with the law of supply and demand, as you guys know it. Most goods are Ordinary goods. As an example, if this packet of chips costs ₹ 50, instead of ₹ 20 right now, what would you do?"

"We would switch to some other packet," suggested Haider.

"No, you better stop eating, look at your belly..." commented Romesh with a grin.

We all shared the laughter.

"Right, so either way, the demand for this specific product will go down with an increase in price, and they would have no way but to get back the demand by reducing the price. That's an Ordinary good for you."

"We always thought that this was the only way it worked in economics. Are all goods not Ordinary goods?"

"No, we are coming to the second type of good, which is the exact opposite of an Ordinary good, called a Giffen Good."

"Giffen good? I am hearing of it for the first time in my life," I accepted my ignorance in front of the master.

"Giffen goods are goods that experience an increase in quantity demanded when price rises, or conversely, a decrease in quantity demanded when the price falls," the Monk explained and paused for a few moments. That was his way of letting us absorb the new knowledge.

"Demand goes up when the prices go up? Is that not shocking? Why would that happen? Why would I want to buy this packet of chips at ₹ 50?"

"Yes, this contradicts the law of supply and demand. But look at it this way. Giffen goods are usually staple goods that don't have any close substitutes. Giffen goods have something unique about them."

"Okay, so you are saying that I might still buy this packet of chips even for ₹ 50 if there was no substitute for it?" I tried to confirm my understanding of Giffen goods.

"Yes, you are right, Manish. Not only that, but I am also going a step ahead and saying that not only would you still buy one packet of the costly ₹ 50 chips, but you will buy more than one packet of these chips even if it were priced at ₹ 50."

This was getting too much for me. When our myths are shattered and when new ideas make a dent on our ego, or when our belief systems that were built over decades are suddenly challenged, our first rection is always to repel any such challenging thought or idea. So, naturally, I resisted.

"No way, I am not going to do that ever in my right mind. Not sure if anyone else would also do that either," I looked around at the other participants. Everyone looked as confused as I was, if not more.

"Okay hold on, Manish, don't rush to conclusions. Imagine that you came here with a budget of ₹ 100 to buy some snacks for your family. You thought that you would buy a ₹ 30 packet of chips and a ₹ 70 pizza from the local shop here, okay?" the Monk was trying his best to explain the idea.

"Okay"

"Now, imagine that ₹ 70 is the lowest price for the pizza available."

"Okay... so?"

"So now, when you come here, you realise that the chips are Rs 50, instead of the regular ₹ 30, and you do not have an alternative to it. You must buy the chips."

"Okay."

"But after buying a packet of the costly chips, you are left with only ₹ 50. You cannot buy a pizza now that you are not left with enough money."

"Okay..."

"So, you have two choices... to go back home with one packet of chips and no pizza and face the consequences of the same, or to buy another packet of chips from the leftover amount. What would you choose?"

There was pin-drop silence. We all knew that we were wrong, but perhaps our egos were stopping us from acknowledging our mistake. Obviously, the Monk understood this and continued.

"Well, it is not that common, though. It doesn't happen everywhere every time, but it does happen, especially for staple goods. An increase in the price of these goods often means consumers are left with less money to buy more expensive products, so they are forced to buy more of the goods, despite the higher price."

"We never thought this could happen. Can you help us with more examples?"

"Sure. Let's look at the demand for rice in South India. Many people in this area are farmers with a low income. A large part of their diet consists of rice because it is cheap, and they cannot afford to buy expensive food. With the money they are left with, they supplement their diet with more expensive food such as meat or other animal products. Now, when the price of rice increases, the poor farmers have less money left to buy more expensive food, so they may be forced to buy more rice instead, in spite of and because of the price of rice going up."

"Wow, buy more because of the higher price... unbelievable, but you are right, it happens."

"Yes, it happens. So, do not make the mistake of trusting the price of the good to assess its worth and assume that the price would be automatically adjusted as per the demand-supply model. Always do your own independent assessment."

"Right, so this statue might be a Giffen good?"

"You see, it may not be easy to identify a Giffen good, and that is why an independent Intrinsic Value assessment is important," commented the Monk.

"Right."

"And then there is a third type of goods called Veblen Goods."

"Wow... we have never even heard of these terms before."

"I know, but that is what you came to this session for, no?"

"Yes, absolutely," we all chorused.

"Right, so back to Veblen goods. Although similar at first glance, Veblen goods also experience increased demand as their price rises. However, they are luxury products – used mainly as status symbols – and not staple goods. Thus, in the case of these goods, the increase in quantity demanded is fuelled by the price itself, because they are mainly bought for conspicuous consumption and not out of necessity."

"So, we are back to the Benz example. Are you saying that, though a Benz surely demands a higher price, it may be priced much more than fair because it's a Veblen good?"

"You are getting there... all I am trying to say via these examples is that you should not trust the price of any good at its face value. Prices of goods can be Veblen or Giffen, and not necessarily Ordinary. You ought to find the true worth, or the true Intrinsic Value of the good."

"Impressive and very interesting."

Sulekha was away while we were discussing the Tri-goods, and she came back with a small packet of almonds for each one of us to munch on.

"Here... you will need this to sharpen your brain so that it can absorb all these new concepts," she said with a smile as she distributed the almonds from the packet she was carrying.

Along with the almonds, she also handed us a set of learning cards.

She continued, "Also, it is important that you keep filling in your learning cards so that you keep registering your lessons in your mind. The Monk and I will be away for a while, though we will be somewhere in the market itself. You guys should make use of this opportunity to sit here on the benches and fill up these cards as you snack. We should be back in twenty minutes or so."

We gladly accepted the almonds and the set of cards, took our seats on the benches inside the mall, and started to fill in our learning cards.

Day 4
Avoid the Traps

WHAT IS SIGN VALUE?

The assumed value of a product because of the prestige (social status) that it imparts upon the possessor.

Learning Card#19

Day 4
Avoid the Traps

WHAT ARE TRI-GOODS?

Not all goods obey the law of demand.

Ordinary goods, Giffen goods, Veblen goods together constitute Tri-goods.

Learning Card#20

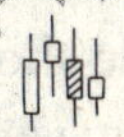

Day 4
Avoid the Traps

WHAT ARE ORDINARY GOODS?

Goods that obey the law of demand. Demand reduces if price of the good goes up.

Most goods are Ordinary goods.

Learning Card#21

Day 4
Avoid the Traps

WHAT ARE GIFFEN GOODS?

These goods do not obey the law of demand. Demand goes up if the price of Giffen goods go up.

Valid for staple goods in specific cases.

Learning Card#22

Day 4
Avoid the Traps

WHAT ARE VEBLEN GOODS?

These goods do not obey the law of demand. Demand goes up if the price of Veblen goods go up.

Valid for luxury goods in specific cases.

Learning Card#23

As I finished my last almond, my pride in my pack of learning cards knew no bounds. There was just so much to learn.

I looked around as some of the participants were still writing. I looked around the mall but could not locate the Monk and Sulekha anywhere.

Most of us were done filling up the cards when the Monk and Sulekha arrived. The chemistry between the two was very confusing to me. They worked so well as a team but I have been observing some kind of friction between the two of late, for reasons I had no clue about.

"Done, team?" inquired Sulekha.

"Yes..." came the chorus.

"Okay Manish, so let us go back to that Buddha statue shop? We are now equipped with the right knowledge and we have an unfinished task at hand," suggested the Monk.

"Yes, I was thinking about it. While we got a good glimpse of Tri-goods, my Buddha statue decision remains pending."

"Yeah, let us go..."

All the participants followed us. Before we entered the shop again, I just summarised my dilemma in front of the entire group.

"So, I understand that the price being quoted by the shopkeeper may or may not be fair. I also understand that price cannot be a true judge of the worthiness of the product since prices can change drastically depending on whether the goods are Ordinary, Veblen or Giffen. So, how do I move ahead with a decision in that case? I do not know what kind of good this statue is."

"Yes, price does not tell you anything about the worthiness of anything," confirmed the Monk.

"So, what will tell us about the worthiness in that case?" inquired Arnab.

"The Intrinsic Value."

"Oh, okay! I read about the Intrinsic Value in a book called *The Autobiography of a Stock*. And I learnt that this is the true value of any given stock. The price of the stock can be very different from the true value of the stock," Harry intervened.

"Absolutely right, Harry. So, that is what we need – the true value of this statue. That value will decide its worthiness. Now that you have read the stock book, can you estimate the true value of this statue?" asked the Monk.

"But Monk, there I had some company-related data points like earnings, debt, assets, growth, etc., which helped me calculate the Intrinsic Value of a stock. But how do I do this here? I have no data points here." Harry seemed confused.

"Yes, we may not be accurate, but with some common sense, we can make a fair judgement. To make a fair judgement, we need to ask the shop owner some questions and collect the required data points. Let me show you how..." And the Monk took the lead in eliciting information from the shopkeeper.

"So, brother... tell me, what is this metal?" the Monk started to interact with the shop owner to try and collect some data points which can enable us to have a fair judgement of the Intrinsic Value of the product we were trying to buy.

"This is brass," responded the shop owner.

"Pure 100 per cent brass?"

"No, brass is mixed with tin and lead, but around 70 per cent brass."

"Okay, what's the guarantee in case it rusts or cracks?"

"There is no guarantee or bills provided for any product here."

"Oh, can I just touch it?"

"Yes..."

The Monk touched it and asked me to feel the weight. He also lifted it and felt the weight.

"It's 1.7 kgs," responded the shopowner when he saw the Monk trying to assess the weight of the statue.

"Oh... thanks for this update. We will let you know," the Monk told the shop owner and took us out of the shop yet again.

"So, guys, I think we have enough data points for now."

"Okay."

He continued, "You see, the positive about this statue is that it is 70 per cent brass, and it looks great aesthetically. The negatives are that there is no warranty or bill. Another big negative is the very low weight of just 1.7 kgs. A statue this size should be more than 10 kg. While the outer is made of brass and other metals, it is either hollow from the inside or made of cheap stuff. So, I would assess the value of this statue as anywhere between ₹ 2,500 and ₹ 5,000."

And he continued, "But remember that this is just my assessment of the Intrinsic Value based on my experiences in life and the weightage I give to all the collected data points. If one of you gives more weight to looks than to weight, then your assessment may be different. I was just trying to show you the process to assess the Intrinsic Value of any product like this."

"Yes, we see such differences in Intrinsic Value calculations for stocks as well. Worldwide, there are different methods to calculate the Intrinsic Value, but each method gives more weight to some factors and less to others. So, even though the same company is being analysed, the Intrinsic Value can show significant variation depending on the method applied," Harry recalled his experience with Intrinsic Value calculations.

"Yes, Harry, you are so right. The Intrinsic Value will depend on who is doing the assessment and what they are looking at from the product."

"Got it... I also feel that ₹ 5000 is the maximum we should pay for this," I told the shopkeeper.

He said no, and we started to walk off.

"Seven thousand, not below that!" he negotiated while we were walking away.

"Okay, six thousand done!" I gave my last bet, and the deal was sealed. I could have negotiated better. Then, the point was the understanding of the second rule of the Quadra Kit, and that was done very well. The Intrinsic Value assessment helped us to be more confident in our dealings, rather than being swayed by the market price.

I took out my credit card and was about to pay.

"Only debit cards or cash, please," said the shopkeeper.

"Okay."

As I was about to scan the QR code and pay via UPI, the Monk interrupted and stopped me.

"This is the time you should be aware of the third rule of the Quadra Kit."

"What?"

"You are not allowed to pay online," came the next shocker from the Monk.

"So, how am I supposed to pay?"

"Cash, only cash."

"Monk, you have become old gen. Do you think anyone carries cash in today's world?" I shot back.

"I am old gen for sure, but I keep learning from the new gen. You don't carry cash, I know that. But you only need to pay in cash. Go and get it from that ATM."

Monk pointed me to the nearest ATM, which was barely a hundred metres away across the road.

"But what's the fun, Monk... there are no charges if I pay via UPI, the payment is instant when I pay via UPI, and it gets deducted from the same account from where you are asking me to withdraw the funds from. I am sorry to say this but I find this inconvenient and old gen."

"Right, it is not about saving on the charges. It is about the feel."

"What feel, Monk?"

"You ought to feel something slipping away from your hands – your hard-earned money. This is the third tool of the Quadra Kit – Pay by Cash."

The Monk continued, "And before you guys start contesting whatever I say, considering me as an old gen, remember that whatever you are learning here in this programme is all proven facts. Nothing being taught here is a new idea or a gut feel. There are multiple scientific studies that you can look up if they give you more faith in the ideas and principles that I am trying to inculcate in you. Convince yourself. But do not ignore anything without researching enough."

The Monk's rules were strange, or they seemed so. But they had been very helpful. And I felt that by now I had enough courage to ask him about the scientific backing of this specific rule.

"Sure, Monk. We will do the research, and we do have faith in you and the programme, and that is precisely why we are here. But, just so that our conviction level goes up one step further, can you please highlight any scientific study for this third tool of the Quadra Kit? Not that we don't trust you. It is just to ensure that we know what we can expect when we research."

"Why should I have any objection, Manish? For this rule, you can search for a survey conducted by IIIT Delhi on the internet. In a gist, approximately 74 per cent of people in India overspend as a result of using UPI and other digital payment methods. As much as 95 per cent found UPI a convenient method for making payments. And remember that convenience triggers indiscipline, which makes the taming of expenses even more difficult."

"Amazing..."

I didn't utter a word after that. I just obeyed the third rule of the Quadra Kit, went across the road, withdrew the cash and paid it to the shop owner. As I counted and paid the cash, I must admit that I didn't feel like paying the bundle of cash. It was indeed my hard-earned money. I didn't feel good at all, and I understood precisely why this third rule existed.

Most of us completed our shopping over the next hour or so and tried to use the three tools of the Quadra Kit as we went around. We were rather hungry by then, and it was turning dark.

"Okay, last fifteen minutes please. We have to leave soon," announced Sulekha.

"But what about the fourth tool?" I asked Varun.

"I think the Monk has missed that."

Meanwhile, Arnab was the last one still shopping. He was looking for something authentic, ethnic and antique, but the market had mostly imported and smuggled stuff.

"Okay, Arnab, leave it if you can't find the right thing..." said Sulekha.

"Aren't you feeling hungry, Arnab?" Vineet shouted.

"Yes, hungry and frustrated as well."

"Why frustrated?"

"Because I just can't find what I am looking for."

"That's okay... what is the compulsion to buy something?" consoled Sulekha.

"There is no compulsion, but just a mix of hunger, frustration and tiredness, I think. We have been roaming for around three hours, and still I can't find any stuff that is worthy enough."

"Okay, guys, everyone on the bus in two minutes, please!" shouted Sulekha.

Arnab was surprised but not amused at this last instruction from Sulekha. We still had fifteen minutes left. He still wanted to check if he could find something. All of us were taken aback by this sudden announcement.

Anyway, we obeyed the orders. Arnab sat all alone in the back of the bus, disappointment writ large on his face.

"I think you missed the last tool of the Quadra Kit. We could have spent fifteen more minutes and learnt that fourth tool while allowing Arnab to complete his shopping. Am I missing something, Sulekha?" questioned Chandra, clearly feeling bad for his friend.

We all had more or less the same thoughts.

"Chandra, note down the fourth tool," instructed Sulekha.

"But we could have allowed him to shop, no? What was the hurry to come back? How desperately he was trying to find a gift, even though he was frustrated and hungry. I mean, we were all hungry, but we were all ready to wait for him," Chandra argued.

Arnab seemed virtually in tears.

"That's exactly what the fourth tool says," mentioned the Monk.

At the back of my mind, I always knew that there was something cooking up, and there was some strong reason behind everything that happened in this programme..

"What does the fourth tool say, Monk? Don't shop?" asked Chandra in a kind of sarcastic tone.

"Yes. Don't shop."

"What does that even mean?" Now Chandra was also getting irritated.

"It means that we should never shop in any extreme emotional state. Hunger, anger, and tiredness are all extreme emotional states. Shopping is strictly prohibited in any such state," announced the Monk.

He continued, "Shopping while feeling particularly famished, tired, or emotional will only lead to making more impulsive purchases than usual. And the reason is simple. You want to get done shopping quickly so that you can then handle your extreme emotions of hunger, anger, or anything else. And this hurried shopping will only lead to irrational decisions and money wastage."

"We just saved you some money, Arnab. Sorry, we had to be a bit harsh, but we are all learning here," Sulekha said and patted his back.

Arnab smiled after a long time.

"Now that we are equipped with all the tools of the Quadra Kit, it is time to move. Move on, Rama," the Monk instructed the bus driver.

Each of us were content and we were looking forward to the dinner at the resort. There were just two 'not so happy' faces in the bus now – the Monk and Sulekha. There was an uneasy calm between them.

Anyway, that one-hour drive from the shopping mall to the resort was breezy. I slept like I hadn't slept for ages, only to be woken up by the squeaking noise made by the brakes of the bus as it arrived at the resort, and later by Varun's patting.

As soon as I woke up, the hunger pangs were back. We went back to our huts, got refreshed and were back at the lawn, where our piping-hot dinner was laid out.

And there were no more discussions at dinner time that night. We just relished the food.

"We miss the home-made lunch we had at your house, Sulekha," I tried to trigger a conversation.

"This is also home-made. Isn't this your home, even if it is only for a limited time?" remarked Sulekha.

"Yes, sure Sulekha. We really respect you a lot for the person you are," I conveyed my feelings to her.

"So nice of you to say that, Manish. I am just an ordinary person like you, but your views about me make me feel good."

"Want some more rice?" Sulekha asked me noticing my empty plate. She really was very caring.

"Yeah, I will get some. Don't worry."

I returned after a refill and saw that Sulekha had left. It was rare for both the Monk and Sulekha to be absent. But then came Abid, one of the assistants and the kitchen manager, and handed over our next set of learning cards to us.

"Sulekha ji asked me to distribute this to all of you. You can fill them after your dinner. She might take a while to be back," he informed us.

We took our cards and sat down to fill them out after dinner.

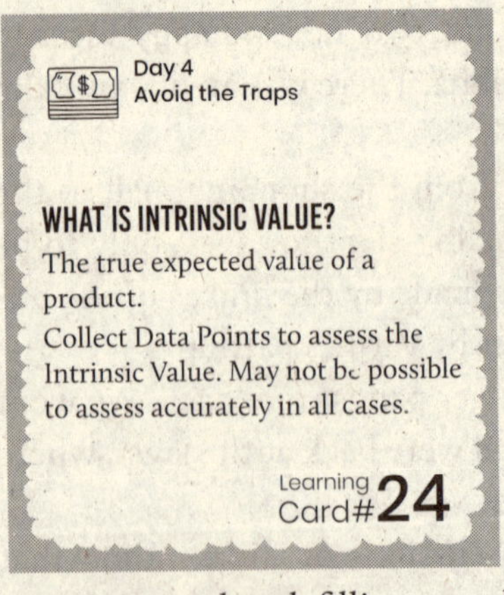

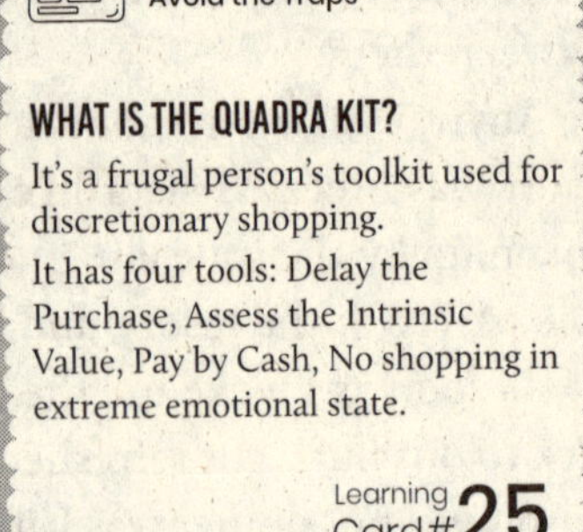

We completed filling our learning cards and were feeling sleepy. But there was no sign of the Monk or Sulekha. This was very unusual.

We were just looking around the resort when I saw Sulekha running out from the Monk's hut. I could see tears running down her face. The huts were not far off, and we could clearly hear the sobbing against the backdrop of silence in the mini jungle.

"What's Sulekha doing in the Monk's hut?" I whispered to Varun.

"No idea, buddy. But why is she crying?" Varun asked a more pertinent question.

"No idea. Has the Monk been rude to her? He doesn't seem like a rude person."

"I am not sure what's happening."

We waited for another fifteen minutes at the dinner lawn hoping that we'd get to see at least one of them, or we'd get an update.

Since neither of them came to the lawn, we decided to retire to our huts.

Day 5

HEDONIC TREADMILL

I woke up from a disturbed sleep the previous night, primarily because of the visuals of a crying Sulekha. It was also our last day at the resort, and we wanted it to end well. It had been such an amazing experience so far.

As I ventured out of the cosiness of nature and the natural warmth of my bed, I happened to glance at the table, and I saw a note which highlighted the tasks for the day. Someone must have kept it while I was asleep.

Sulekha's absence was intriguing, but we had to pull ourselves up and focus on the tasks at hand, the first of which was to go and water the plants. We had done it many times now, and we were aware of what exactly was required to be done. Fill up the cans, trek up, start watering, and get back.

It was all done and dusted in an hour or so. While this task was naturally very satisfying, it didn't seem creative enough. I was glad I did what I did, but I wouldn't be excited for another such watering trip if asked to do it again.

I sat with Varun after we came back, and he agreed with my views on the lack of excitement of watering plants. Maybe because, trees were not our passion. We all need to actually discover our individual passion areas. Anyway, as per the schedule, we headed for breakfast. The Monk was understandably absent since he was not a breakfast guy, but we were all glad to see Sulekha, and that too at her cheerful best.

"Good morning, Sulekha! How are you?" I could not resist asking her.

"I am good, Manish; I hope you slept well."

"Not really, but that is okay. Glad to see you here."

"Where else would I go?" Sulekha smiled back while she started to greet Haider and Harry, who were coming to join us for breakfast.

Over the next fifteen minutes, everyone arrived.

"Okay, team, did anyone collect the number cards that were kept randomly along the trees you watered this morning?" announced Sulekha.

"Number cards? What's that? I didn't find any," I responded.

While a few other participants supported what I said, we also saw Romesh and Arnab showing the number cards they had collected.

"Show me what they are like," I requested Romesh.

I looked at them and tried to recollect if I had seen anything like that in the morning while watering the trees, but could not recollect. Neither could Varun.

"We could not find such cards anywhere, Sulekha. Also, we were not aware that we were supposed to collect anything like this while watering the plants."

"That is okay, Manish. These number cards were strategically located at random points, and only those who were excited and happy about watering the plants could locate them. So, for most of you, this activity did not give you much happiness, at least not the same as the first day. Agree?"

We were speechless. And we naturally wondered as to how she knew what we had been thinking or discussing all this while? Was everyone thinking the way we were? Why had the excitement gone down for the same task that sounded no less than life elevating, noble and worthy just a few days back?

"I agree, Sulekha, and I am sure many of us would. We were glad we did the watering, but if you ask us to keep doing this task for the rest of our lives, we cannot. It is not exciting enough. It is not satisfying enough," I responded.

"Thank you for being so candid. But don't worry. It is not your mistake. It is in your genes," mentioned Sulekha.

"Genes? What is in our genes, Sulekha?"

"Being happy or not..." she responded casually. Just like with the Monk, her responses triggered inquisitiveness, and that was one of the keys to learning new ideas.

"I am totally confused now, Sulekha. What does that even mean when you say that being happy or not is in our genes, and what does this have to do with being excited while watering the plants?"

"Let us pick up our breakfast plate as we discuss this very interesting topic of the day that can help you all save a significant amount of money and create massive wealth," remarked Sulekha.

We went about the mini buffet very well understanding the fact that there would be no buffet from the next day. This was our last day in this beautiful, peaceful, and natural place.

As we gathered around Sulekha, she started to talk about the day's topic.

"See, each one of us has a genetic set point of happiness. It could be different for different people but for one person, it is generally baselined by our genes."

"Genetic set point? Means what? I do feel varying levels of happiness throughout the day. So, what do you mean that there is a set point for happiness?" I countered.

"Yes, I agree with Manish," responded Varun.

Varun continued, “I remember feeling joyous when I had got my last salary raise, when we had gone to Thailand, and when we had had our first child. There were so many incidents when we felt sad as well, especially when we lost close relatives in our family. So, a set point of happiness seems strange,” Varun supported my point.

“You were, I am sure,” responded Sulekha.

“So, what is your message about this so-called happiness set point?”

“You were very happy, and you were very sad. But what are you right now?” Sulekha asked an open question while looking at Varun and me.

“Well, we are kind of neutral right now,” Varun responded.

“See, that is the whole point. This is what I am trying to say. Are you as happy as you were when your salary was raised? Or when your wife gave birth to your daughter, or when you went on an international trip?” asked Sulekha.

“No, of course not. And that is natural, no?” I responded.

“Yes, it is natural, and so is the happiness set point, which is naturally decided by your genes,” mentioned Sulekha.

“Can you please elaborate, Sulekha?” Harry intervened.

“Look at it like this. You are as happy today as you were before the pay raise, apart from short time volatility in between. Does that make more sense?”

“Hmmm... maybe... like the stock market and Intrinsic Value?” commented Harry, again sharing his experience from the stock book that he claimed to have read, and was always excited to talk about.

“Absolutely bang on, Harry. In between the bears and bulls of the market, the price of a stock does return to the Intrinsic Value of that stock at some point.”

Sulekha was no dud with stock investments as well. How come everyone here seemed to know everything? Anyways, this was not the time to harp on the wisdom of the staff in this resort, but to understand the new animal called happiness set point.

"And the Intrinsic Value is the happiness set point that you are mentioning?" asked Harry.

"Yes, and just like Intrinsic Value is different for each stock, the happiness set point is different for each one of you," assured Sulekha.

"Interesting. So, you are saying that each of us has a unique, genetically determined set point, or baseline level of happiness?" I asked.

"Absolutely, Manish. But be aware that while a stock price may take years to come back to its Intrinsic Value, the happiness set point is far more efficient. Our happiness reverts to the set point fairly quickly, usually within a matter of days, if not hours."

This was one of the most life-elevating discussions I ever had. It was like a revelation. Why didn't I read about this earlier? Why does no one talk about these things?

"I have a question, Sulekha. If we all have a pre-determined happiness set point, why didn't the salary increment excite me at all?" asked Kavita.

"That is quite possible, Kavita. Your set point is different from Manish's, and his set point is different from Haider's, and so on. Just like the Intrinsic Value of a stock, the happiness set point is unique to every individual. Some are happy with very little, and some are unhappy with a lot. It is in your genes."

"Hmmm... interesting," mentioned Kavita as she seemed satisfied with Sulekha's response.

"And this journey of life is like the sinusoidal wave of an alternating current. Happiness levels may keep going up and down, but they will keep reverting to our natural genetic set point. It is like being on a treadmill. No matter how much you move, you stay in the same place in terms of your happiness levels," explained Sulekha.

And she continued to dive deeper and plough back her wisdom to all of us. "And because of this analogy with a treadmill, we call this entire idea of varying happiness levels and reverting to the set point Hedonic Treadmill, or a pleasure treadmill."

"Hedonic Treadmill?" I asked curiously.

"Yes, this Hedonic Treadmill is the empirically supported idea that whatever happens in our lives to increase or decrease our happiness level, our happiness will soon return to its set point. When we get a promotion, get divorced, have kids, or experience any other notable gain or loss in our lives, we get an initial spike – either positive or negative – in our happiness level. However, as time goes on, the feeling of happiness or sadness caused by the change in conditions starts to dissipate until we're back around our genetic set point of happiness."

"So, are you saying that there is no permanent happiness increase or decrease away from our genetic set point?" I inquired.

"You are generally right. Nothing external can dislodge your genetic set point. People, situations, objects nothing," clarified Sulekha.

"Really?" I was unable to believe all this.

"This has been proven as well. There was an event wherein lottery winners were invited, and their views were taken. The group of lottery winners reported being similarly happy before and after winning the lottery and were also expected to have a similar level of happiness in a couple of years. These findings show that having a large monetary gain had no effect on their baseline level of happiness, for both present and expected happiness in the future." Sulekha was trying her best to explain the intricacies of the Hedonic set point.

Arnab finally asked the question that I had been wanting to ask for a while.

"I get what you say, Sulekha, and this topic is really very interesting. But I am just wondering if this has anything to do with the art of saving money."

By this time, we were all done with our breakfast, but none of us wanted to get up to keep our plates. We could not afford to miss this discussion.

"Everything..." responded Sulekha, and she continued with utmost confidence and elegance in her voice, "The Hedonic Treadmill has everything to do with the art of saving money."

"How?" asked Arnab.

"Once you understand the Hedonic Treadmill, you also understand that the pleasures that you are trying to buy with your money will definitely not have a lasting or permanent effect. The new curtains, the new car, a new laptop, a new version of the gadget – nothing is going to give you a lasting happiness upgrade, because it just cannot. Your happiness levels are genetic. This vital understanding helps you keep yourself away from the herd and save more rather than spending on upgrades and enhancements in life that may not be needed at all."

"So, what are we running after then, if we are always going to be happy as per our genetic set point?" asked Arnab.

"Everything is futile, man!" exclaimed Chandra.

"Nothingness is all we need..." added Kulwant.

And with everyone sharing their spiritual comments about the Hedonic Treadmill, we all laughed and relaxed a bit, just trying to get the idea to sink in and its massive possible impact on our life and lifestyle.

This was a game changer. This could help us avoid the herd. In fact, I suddenly began to pity all my colleagues at the workplace who worked so hard and went through such stress to earn money and then would spend that money to buy the latest gadget or a big car. I wish they knew that those things were not going to change their happiness level even by an iota. It was all preset in the genes.

Sulekha got up to keep her breakfast plate, and we all followed her one by one.

"Okay, let us take an hour's break – your last break in this resort, and then reassemble here at the same place. I have an important announcement to make. Also, we will continuc our discussions and answer unanswered questions about the Hedonic Treadmill. Does that sound good?" announced Sulekha.

"Yes, sure..." we all nodded in chorus.

"And do fill up the learning cards when you go back to your huts," instructed Sulekha, as she took her leave.

Varun and I walked back to our huts – happier than when we had here in the morning. We had learnt something new. Perhaps, that was the idea of being happy – learning new stuff every moment.

And the first thing we did when we got back to our huts was to fill up the learning cards on our tables.

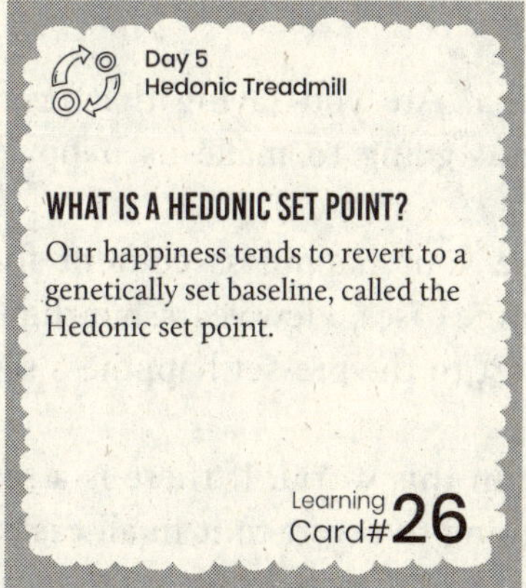

After filling up the learning cards, Varun and I kept discussing the Hedonic set point for a long time. We went back to our respective lives and remembered how the excitement of a new car, or a gadget got neutralised in days, how the sadness of the loss of a loved one also got neutralised in a few weeks or months. We were just in awe of this concept. If we build enough conviction in the Hedonic Treadmill, we can save ourselves from the mindless race of consumption.

We reassembled at the lawn after about an hour, as instructed. Sulekha and the other participants joined as well.

But where was the Monk? We hadn't seen him since the previous day. What was going on? It was our last day, and he was not to be seen anywhere.

"So, where were we?" asked Sulekha.

"Arnab was asking about the futility of doing anything in life if our happiness is pre-decided by a genetic set point," I tried to kickstart the discussion and handed over the baton to Arnab.

"Yes, right..." Arnab confirmed.

"So, if nothing else can make us happy, then why save more? For our freedom?" Arnab threw an additional question at Sulekha.

"No..." responded Sulekha and raised everyone's eyebrows yet again.

"What are you saying, Sulekha? Are you saying that even achieving financial freedom is not going to make us happy?" Arnab asked the obvious.

"Freedom will surely increase your happiness content for some time, maybe months or in some cases, a few years, but then, now you know, that you will revert to the pre-set happiness set point soon after."

"So, then everything is futile in this world. If there is a set point of happiness, and we are going to revert to it in all cases, then what is the fun of achieving any goal in life, whether freedom or anything else?" I interrupted.

This discussion was getting extremely interesting. And Sulekha was handling it so well that, surprisingly, we were not missing the Monk and his wisdom. Yes, we were all curious to know about his whereabouts, but Sulekha was as good as anyone else.

"Achieving goals is not the ultimate goal," remarked Sulekha.

And again, there was a pin-drop silence – a silence so dead that we could hear our breathing.

"Sulekha, your one-liners are killers. Please help us understand this. What does it mean that our goal is not the goal?" asked Haider.

"Sure. You see, the goal is never the goal, but the journey towards a worthy goal is the goal. It's that process, that journey that keeps you happy. If you enjoy climbing, then reaching the top is not going to give you lasting happiness, but the enjoyment of climbing will. Similarly, your financial freedom is a worthy goal, but the journey towards freedom and the journey after it, is what you are going to derive daily happiness from – the learning, the failures, the setbacks, the getting back up, the fight, the skill creation – all along until you get there. Those give you the dopamine you need," Sulekha clarified.

"But Monk and you have a goal to plant so many trees. What do you have to say about that?" asked Arnab.

"Yes, that's a worthy goal. But my happiness is derived from the process of watering them every single day, acquiring knowledge about different tree species, learning to propagate them, caring for them, curing their diseases, protecting them, replacing them when there is a setback... the entire process is what gives happiness and keeps us close to our Hedonic set point."

"Yes, life is a journey and not a destination," concluded Arnab.

"So, are you saying that money is not important, since the happiness set point is fixed? So, should we stop earning money?" I ventured out once again.

"Money is important, of course, for your happiness, but only as far as your basic needs of food, clothing, shelter and freedom are concerned."

"Ah, you also consider freedom a basic need?" I asked.

"Yes, it has often been underestimated, but it is very difficult for a person to stay happy without meeting these four basic needs," remarked Sulekha.

She continued, "After your basic needs are met, it is your set point that matters, and trying to stay close to the set point by reducing volatility is what will increase the overall happiness content in life. Avoid unnecessary spending on things that excite you, unless, of course, they are a need. A Benz is not a need, but a car is. In the excitement of a Benz, you might delay your freedom, one of your four basic needs. And since the excitement of the Benz will revert back to the set point anyway, a second-hand car can also do the same job as a new one."

"Interesting... as they say, fill your life with experiences, not things. Have stories to tell, not stuff to show," I commented.

"So, my take is that freedom will allow us to work on what we love. And that work will keep us close to the Hedonic set point. It will help us avoid unnecessary volatility in our happiness content and make us feel more content and fulfilled. The rest that excite us are just part of the herd. They are better avoided. Freedom and Happiness are all we want, and a herd usually lacks both," remarked Haider.

I thought he summed it up pretty well.

While we seemed to be concluding the Hedonic set point discussion, we heard a fast-approaching ambulance siren. Sulekha got up immediately and directed the ambulance towards the Monk's hut. They rushed along with a stretcher and other first aid supplies.

We were taken aback by this sudden development.

"Someone must have called the ambulance, right?" I whispered to Varun.

"It must have been Sulekha. The Monk must be unwell," responded Varun.

Then we saw the Monk being taken away on a stretcher, accompanied by the ambulance staff and Sulekha. After seeing the ambulance off, Sulekha came back and joined us.

Before any of us could ask the obvious question, she clarified, "We knew about the complications many months ago. Now, he just has a few days to live... a week maximum," said Sulekha in a matter-of-fact manner.

"What?"

"What is wrong with him?"

"Is he so seriously unwell?"

All of us were numb with shock. We suddenly felt a loss of energy, an emptiness, a shock – as if we were losing a close family member.

"Yeah," confirmed Sulekha.

She was still composed and calm. To be fair, she must have known the state of the Monk's health for a long time. But nothing had been disclosed to us. And who would have guessed with all the activities he had been part of with us?

"But what happened to him?" I asked.

"He has a last-stage brain tumour. The fact that he survived this long is a testimony to his discipline and focus on things that made him happy," clarified Sulekha.

"Oh man! Why did no one tell us? And why did all of you conduct this session? What was the need?" asked Haider.

"That was the Monk's wish. It had to be honoured," confirmed Sulekha, her eyes welling up.

Most of us were still speechless and were trying to recover from the shock.

"But at least the Monk could have rested in such a case. I mean, you are good enough to conduct these sessions, Sulekha," I commented.

"He didn't want to," clarified Sulekha.

"But why?"

"He said he is doing what he loves the most – teaching the art of saving money, planting trees, and so on, and therefore, didn't go to the hospital earlier. He wanted to live all his days to the fullest."

We were amazed. We had no more questions, and we were in even more awe of this great man who had lived his life fully until the last day.

It was almost lunchtime. The staff had already started making arrangements for lunch as if it were a regular day. They were surely already aware of the Monk's health.

We were all still in a state of shock.

"So, is that why you were crying last night and didn't come out after dinner?" I dared to finally ask Sulekha.

"Yes. The Monk knew that yesterday was probably the last night he could consciously communicate with me. And he did try his best to reinforce the message he always believed in."

"And is it okay for you to tell us what his message was?" Varun asked.

"Nothing new for me. He wanted me to continue with this programme and ensure that the trees get watered and the animals get fed. He blessed me, hugged me, kissed my hands, and then peacefully went to sleep. I was there for some time, watching him sleep. I was hoping he would wake up just one more time, one last time. I really wish so. But that was not to be..."

Sulekha began sobbing. We didn't want to disturb her any further, so we sat quietly letting her express her emotions.

She gathered herself and said, "I will be winding up the session, and then we can all pack our stuff and move back to the city. The bus will drop us there. I will be with the Monk at the hospital for the remaining few days of his life. He has no one else. You guys can head home."

"Do you need any help from us, Sulekha?"

"No, thanks. You have all been so good. Really, thank you!" she said, fighting back her tears.

"So, will we ever have any such sessions in future?"

"Why not? The Monk's mission will continue. I will try to take it forward. That is what he always wanted."

"That is nice to know, Sulekha."

I was also relieved that Sulekha had something to look forward to in life, especially considering her relations with her spouse, and the Monk's state. She had a mission to work on and a purpose which gave happiness.

"Okay, guys, before we break, for one last time, let us all try and collectively recount some of our key learnings from the session. I will take a recording of this, and if luck gives me a chance, I will show it to the Monk when I meet him in the hospital. Okay, let's go... no rules this time..." said an emotional Sulekha as she handed over her phone to one of the assistants there while switching on the video camera.

"Okay, yes, first learning..." she kick-started our train of thought.

"Life is all about being happy... this is what I learnt today," started Harry.

"Yes, it's not even about making anyone happy, because you can't give anything unless you have it yourself. Right, but where do we find our happiness?" asked Sulekha.

"It is in our journey... our journey to attain something," I responded.

"Excellent, it is not in the goal or the end product. It is always in the journey... the process. So proud of you, Manish. Come, give me a hug."

I hugged Sulekha. She seemed sad and happy at the same time.

"Don't worry about my tears, guys. I will bounce back to my Hedonic set point," she had a strange smile on her tear-stained face. "And how does our journey become worthy of happiness?" Sulekha gave the next trigger for one of us to respond and reaffirm what we had learnt.

"When the goal is beautiful..." mentioned Varun.

"Absolutely."

"And what enables us to choose beautiful goals?"

"Most worthy goals are not monetarily rewarding. Hence, financial freedom allows us to choose our true and worthy goals," suggested Kavita.

"Excellent, Kavita. What helps us achieve financial freedom quickly?"

"Saving money..." Haider was very prompt in his response.

"Great Haider, and what helps us save even more money faster?"

"Learning the art of saving money," Romesh chipped in as well.

"Yes, that is why you all attended this session. And what is the idea behind learning the art of saving money?"

"Saving more is a factor of our mind, rather than of any Excel sheets or mobile apps. When we understand our behaviour and response to various microeconomic concepts, we understand how our mind misbehaves with us, and thus, it becomes easier to tame our mind, and thus save more," explained Chandra

"Beautiful Chandra. You nailed it!" responded Sulekha as she opened her arms, inviting Chandra to give her a hug. Chandra obliged.

"I wish you all the very best in life."

She hugged each one of us individually for one last time.

We had a group photo with all the participants, Sulekha and the entire resort staff. There was only one person missing from the group, but his memories were etched forever in our minds.

I took a solo with Sulekha as well, and also got some of my learning cards autographed by her. I gave her one last hug. I also had tears in my eyes. We were departing as if we were losing a family member in Sulekha.

The Money Monk had had a lasting impression on us, but Sulekha was the new Money Monk, and more than deserving.

Ten years later

THE MISSION LIVES ON

This was the session by Money Monk, that Varun and I attended almost ten years ago which changed our outlook towards our understanding of the Secret Alpha. The session ended more than a decade back but it continues to occupy our mind spaces, and our discussions more often than not.

Both of us have come a long way in our lives. We got financially free, and have been able to chase our respective passions.

Kritika and I work very hard even today, but it never feels like work anymore since we are working on our passion. We have a consulting company where we mentor young couples in leading a happy, satisfied, and enriching married life. Our aim is to reduce the divorce rate in our country. Both of us felt connected to this dream, and love innovating our course content, meeting new couples in our sessions, learn from their experiences, and in the process keep learning ourselves – thus adding more to the quality of our own happy married life.

Not that we earn too much money from this initiative, but who cares about money after having achieved financial freedom? We have all our basic needs already fulfilled, and we understand that there is no upper limit, and that we need to avoid the herd. We appreciate that we have more than enough. We work at our own pace, with the people we like, in the time and days we like. Freedom is truly beautiful.

Varun and Sneha opened a bakery close to their home. Sneha was always a good baker, and Varun was a good salesperson. They seemed to be made for such a business. Freedom allowed both of them to discover their true strengths and work on those, thus increasing the happiness content in their lives.

Varun and I keep meeting often.

Today, we were meeting for a coffee after quite a few weeks.

We were super excited about this meeting because it was not only the two of us this time, but we also had a special third guest, none other than Sulekha. She was in this part of the city and made it a point to connect. We were more than glad.

And finally, we met.

"It is amazing to see you, Sulekha. And I must say that you haven't changed even a bit. You are just the way you were a decade back," I hugged Sulekha while appreciating her agelessness.

"Thank you, but you guys don't look the same," replied Sulekha.

We paused for a while, and then she said, "You guys look younger than you were when you were with us at the resort."

We laughed out loud. Sulekha was still as sharp-witted in her responses as always.

"If you think we look younger, it is courtesy of the freedom we enjoy today, and this freedom would have been nearly impossible without you and the Monk. By the way, we didn't hear about the Monk after the last day of our session."

"Monk passed away before I could reach the hospital that evening. I could not even show him the video and pictures that we took on the last day."

"Oh, that is sad."

There was a pin-drop silence and an uneasy calm among all three of us as our memories jogged through some of the cherished moments with the Monk – the jogging at the beach, the tree plantation, the races, his meditation – everything was just a memory now. Time is the biggest asset we all have. Once it is up, everything else doesn't matter.

"What will you have, Sulekha? Cappuccino?" I asked, trying to interject the beautiful, yet painful memories of the Monk.

"Yes, sure," confirmed Sulekha.

"How are the sessions on the art of saving money going nowadays?" asked Varun.

"Monk's legacy lives on even after he has gone," responded Sulekha.

"Passion lives longer than all of us," she added.

There was depth in every sentence she spoke.

"And how have you guys been?"

"Happy..." was a response that shot from both Varun and me in unison.

"You are the most successful people I have met in the world," responded Sulekha.

"We do not know whether we are successful or not. But we are surely happy with what we do."

"That is why I say that you are the most successful. Because success is nothing but happiness. Happiness is the end objective of every goal in life, and I can see that on both your faces. You guys are brimming with happiness."

"Thank you," I acknowledged.

Our beverages were served. As we picked up our coffee, we toasted to some of the most beautiful and memorable days spent together.

"But I tell you, Sulekha, it was not easy to save money. I mean, the art of saving money gave us the right mindset, but adapting our lives to that mindset was very tough," said Varun.

"Absolutely... we had many uncomfortable conversations with our spouses, and even with our children. It was not easy at all," I agreed.

"Were you looking for easy things in life?" shot back Sulekha.

Varun and I looked at each other and, as always, she read our minds and said,

"Nothing worthwhile is easy in life – not even saving money. Do not ever strive for easy things. Strive for things that make your life worthy, however difficult those might be."

It was clear that Sulekha had not yet lost her knack for life, and was crystal clear on life's most intriguing concepts. Of course, she was the Monk now. And she was so right. Today, we realise the worthiness of those difficult conversations we had with our families. All those sacrifices seem so worthy.

The Art of Saving Money helped us transition to our freedom with relatively less difficulty.

Both Varun and I looked at each other and smiled.

"Yes, it is surely worthy of the effort," we confirmed.

We kept chatting with Sulekha for hours. We never realised when the time passed by, and it was time for her to depart yet again.

We bid goodbye to Sulekha as she left in her cab.

Varun and I came back and sat on our seats. We didn't talk to each other as we were engrossed in our own thoughts. The sun was setting. And it was time for us to leave as well.

One by one, each one of us will lose our companions. We will be all alone. We do not know when our time will be up, and we will have to say good bye to everyone.

But until that time, it is important that we live our life to the fullest, doing what we love doing.

If freedom is what will help us, we must go for it – with full vigour. It is tough but more than worthy. And it is our prime responsibility in life to strive for our freedom and happiness.

The Art of Saving Money is what will get you there faster and safer. Saving money and freedom is not a choice, but a necessity to lead a fulfilling life.

Parting Notes

GET GOING WITH YOUR SECRET ALPHA

Congratulations to you for having read this complete book and reaching this point. Of course, there are so many lessons that you must have learnt while turning its pages.

But hold on. Did you really learn, or did you just read them? And did you agree with them?

Answer a few honest questions before you keep this book away, and move on to pick up another bestseller to trigger your body's dopamine.

Will your wealth or your life change by reading the book? I am sure you must have read other books as well. Has your life changed so far? Will it change now? Of course, you get excited after reading a good book, but don't you fall back into the same routine just after a few hours of reading the book?

Sure, books have a potential to transform lives, but at the end of the day, a book's potential is just what it is – potential, and potential is never real. Does 'reading' books help or does 'absorbing' books help is the question to think about.

By now, you are smart enough to understand that any amount of reading is not going to help you if you are not absorbing the content into your life with concrete changes in your life.

It does not matter how much content we read, but how much gets 'absorbed' in our real life. That is what is going to transform our life.

What transforms our life is not how much content we read, but what how much we are ultimately able to take in, how much we are able to absorb.

So, all the preachings from the Monk about Diderot Trap, Frugality, Herd mentality, Hedonic Treadmill among the others, are only good to the extent they are implemented in our life. If, after reading whatever the Monk taught, we go off to shop for an expensive gadget just because almost everyone around us has it, then we did surely read a lot, but the absorption of the content was low.

A natural question that takes this discussion forward is what will help us increase our reading absorption? What is going to help the majority of the content get in and get implemented in our lives? What is the Secret Alpha to absorb the contents of any book?

My experience shows that there are two things that need to be done to exponentially increase the absorption of our reading content, and these two things are your Secret Alpha from here on.

Secret Alpha 1: Decide

The first Secret Alpha is to be **decisive** about the learnings from the book. Even before you close this book, you need to be decisive of what you have learnt from the book. It could be multiple things, but I would prefer if it is just one thing.

Whatever it is, but be sure of something that you truly wish to adopt in your life. You could mark it in the book right away or you could note it down separately. But do this before you close this book, else the chances are that it might never happen.

It could be something more encompassing like "I want to prepare my financial freedom plan because that can give me true freedom", or "I will never follow the herd because it is harmful for me."

It could also be something small and specific like "I want to follow the Tri-check before my next grocery shopping", or "I want to make sure that I counter the Snackwell Effect by regularly checking for consumption of energy-efficient devices in my home.

Or anything else you feel is important. Be decisive.

Secret Alpha 2: Act

The second Secret Alpha to increase the absorption is that you are going to take **urgent action** on whatever decision you have taken – an action that is going to get you moving in your intended direction.

You are not going to wait until tomorrow or until the weekend. You have to take some action right now. So, if your decision was to prepare a financial freedom plan, you need to send an email to someone who can help you, or you need to talk to a friend who has done this before, or you need to open an Excel sheet where you can start dabbing some numbers to get going.

If your decision was to avoid the herd, then adapt one change that you are going to bring from today that takes you in that direction. It could be wearing that old watch to your workplace tomorrow rather than ordering the new one you were planning to. It could be cancelling your decision to buy a new car and getting the current one overhauled.

If your decision was to follow the Tri-check before going for your next grocery shopping, then jot down the checklist and paste it on your fridge door right now.

It could be anything that gets you moving in the right direction.

Taking **decisive and urgent action is our Secret Alpha** to absorb the learnings from the Money Monk, ultimately leading to a transformed and beautiful life.

Wishing you all the best

My Commitment to You

I am passionate about YOU. I am committed to YOU. It is my life's mission to elevate my society, in whatever way I can.

As with all my other books, this book comes with a 100 per cent commitment to help you, guide you and mentor you on your journey. We will walk this journey together.

You have an absolute right to connect with me, and I will be more than delighted to help you elevate your life.

Official Website:	https://www.manoj-arora.com
ELITE Programme*:	https://elite.manoj-arora.com
Elevate Newsletter:	https://elevate.manoj-arora.com
Blog:	https://elevate-your-life.blogspot.com/
Email:	help@manoj-arora.com
WhatsApp:	+91-9871133619

*ELITE Programme for Financial Freedom: On demand, we designed a unique programme, which we have been running with unmatched success since 2018. Herein, we shortlist a limited set of passionate financial freedom seekers (via an interview process) thrice a year. I personally coach each selected seeker and take them to financial freedom by a defined date.

Annexure

KEY MICROECONOMIC TERMS

Diderot Trap: Acquiring any new possession usually leads to a spiralling consumption. Our mind gets stuck in a Diderot Trap. Be aware and look out for spiralling consumption patterns to alert your mind in time.

Family Inflation: It is the annual inflation of expenses for your family. It can be drastically different from the inflation of your neighbour's family and also from the government-issued inflation figures. It depends on the major expense heads of your family.

Frugality: Frugality is an often-criticised idea of saving money. However, the criticism is primarily triggered by a lack of understanding of the idea of being frugal. A frugal person is often confused with a miser. A miser keeps hoarding money with no upper limit. A frugal person understands the upper limit. A miser doesn't want to spend on anything. A frugal person is wise enough to understand where to spend and where to save. A frugal is wiser, smarter, and more efficient.

Giffen Goods: They are the goods that do not obey the law of demand. In such goods, the demand goes up if the price of Giffen goods go up. This is usually valid for staple goods in very specific cases.

Herd Mentality: Following the herd is a natural mechanism in humans for sense of safety in times of fear. It is not healthy for individuals in normal times to follow the herd. The top of the herd is a moving goalpost and gives us a feeling of having never been able to achieve our goal in spite of our best efforts. Looking up, towards the herd, and moving forward in life is a stressful activity.

Hedonic Treadmill: Our happiness tends to revert to a genetically set baseline, called the Hedonic set point. In spite of our best efforts to spike our happiness content, our happiness levels tend to revert to the Hedonic set point. It is like running on a Hedonic Treadmill.

Induced Consumption: Induced Consumption is a consumption that is induced for various reasons. It drives Lifestyle Inflation. Induced consumption is a result of increased income and herd mentality.

Induced Demand – Lewis-Mogridge Position: Abundance or availability of goods leads to increase in its consumption. This is a demand which is induced just because of over availability of products. While shopping, be watchful and stay focused on your needs. Induced Demand is also called the Lewis-Mogridge Position.

Intrinsic Value: It is the true expected value of a product. We may need to collect data points to assess the Intrinsic Value of any product. It may not be possible to assess the Intrinsic Value accurately in all cases.

Lifestyle Inflation: The appreciation in lifestyle of an individual or a family as a result of increased income or savings is called Lifestyle Inflation. Induced consumption is the microeconomic theory that drives Lifestyle Inflation.

Moving Goalpost: It refers to a situation where the criteria of any specific goal is changed while on the way towards the goal. Imagine a soccer game where the goalposts keep shifting. A Moving goalpost can be extremely frustrating and stressful.

Ordinary Goods: Those goods which obey the law of supply and demand are called Ordinary goods. The demand for Ordinary goods reduces if the price of such goods goes up. Most goods that you deal with in day-to-day life are Ordinary goods.

Quadra Kit: It's a frugal person's toolkit used for discretionary shopping. It has four tools namely: Delay the purchase, Assess the Intrinsic Value, Pay By Cash, No Shopping in extreme emotional state.

Self-Monitoring: The idea behind self-monitoring is that anything that is tracked, improves. We do not need anyone to monitor us for our improvements. The tracking must be visible in front of our eyes. The improvement may not be linear, but it works every single time.

Snackwell Effect: As per this effect, any increase in product efficiency leads to increase in its consumption, thus negating the impact of efficiency gains.

Sign Value: It is the assumed value of a product because of the prestige (social status) that it imparts upon the possessor.

Tri-Check: It is a three-step process involving inventory check, shopping list preparation, and sticking to the list, which saves time, money, and energy while shopping for repeated items. Seemingly small and simple savings lead to massive gains when compounded over time.

Tri-Goods: Not all goods obey the law of supply and demand. Ordinary goods, Giffen goods, and Veblen goods together constitute Tri-goods.

Veblen Goods: These goods do not obey the law of supply and demand. Demand goes up if the price of Veblen goods goes up. Veblen goods are similar to Giffen goods, the only difference being that these are typically valid for luxury goods in very specific cases, while Giffen goods are mostly for staple goods.